The Best *Wom*
of

M000017254

Smith and Kraus *Books For Actors*
THE MONOLOGUE SERIES

YOUNG ACTOR SERIES

SCENE STUDY SERIES

If you require pre-publication information about upcoming Smith and Kraus books, you may receive our semi-annual catalogue, free of charge, by sending your name and address to *Smith and Kraus Catalogue, 4 Lower Mill Road, North Stratford, NH 03590. Or call us at (800) 895-4331, fax (603) 643-6431.*

The Best
Women's Stage Monologues
of 2000

edited by Jocelyn A. Beard

MONOLOGUE AUDITION SERIES

A SMITH AND KRAUS BOOK

Published by Smith and Kraus, Inc.
177 Lyme Road, Hanover, NH 03755
www.SmithKraus.com

Copyright © 2002 by Smith and Kraus, Inc.
All rights reserved
Manufactured in the United States of America

First Edition: June 2002
10 9 8 7 6 5 4 3 2 1

cover illustration by Lisa Goldfinger
cover and text design by Julia Hill Gignoux

The Monologue Audition Series
ISSN 1067-134X
ISBN 1-57525-287-2

NOTE: These scenes are intended to be used for audition and class study; permission is not required to use the material for those purposes. However, if there is a paid performance of any of the scenes included in this book, please refer to the permissions acknowledgment pages 107–113 to locate the source who can grant permission for public performance.

CONTENTS

Dedicated to the Victims of September 11, 2001

Alaska
Le Wilhelm

Scene: An empty house in central Florida
Serio-Comic
Nadine (thirties to forties), a country pop singer.

> *On her way to a gig, Nadine drops off a sewing machine and some fabric at her new neighbors' house. When her blue Dolly Parton wig draws an appreciative stare or two, she explains that she's got to wear a lot of makeup under the lights or she washes out.*

NADINE: What do you think of the wig? Does it look okay?

I just bought it. I don't usually wear wigs, but I thought, "What the hell?" Got it on sale for $15.95 down at Bruce's Wigs. He's a real dear. You'd love him. I hope you all don't get the wrong impression about me. I don't usually wear this much makeup, especially not this much mascara, but when you're performing, the lights just wash you out something awful. 'Specially my eyes, and my eyes aren't my best feature — my legs are my best feature — but you don't sing with your legs. Least I don't. And unless I put on lots of mascara to bring them out, they're just sort of two blobs. But with the mascara, sometimes people even mention them. Now if I had eyes like Blue, that'd be a different story. But Lydia, ain't that always the way it is? Men got features that they don't really need, and us women could really use them, but we don't have 'em. Someone else always has what I want. Not that I wish I had your eyes and you had mine. I'm not coveting. I wish I had eyes like yours and you had even prettier ones. Whatever you want.

Alaska
Le Wilhelm

Scene: An empty house in central Florida
Dramatic
Nadine (thirties to forties), a country pop singer.

Nadine has dropped by her neighbors' house to discover that her new friend Lydia has just stabbed a strange man with a pair of scissors. When Nadine threatens to call the police, Lydia puts the scissors in her hand and forces her to stab the man several times following which she breaks down into a state of exhausted confusion.

NADINE: *(Indicating the meal she brought for them.)* It's all cold, I'm sure. Cold. I thought it'd be a nice snack. When I was a child, too old not to know better, on Easter morning, we used to . . . I used to hunt eggs . . . brightly colored . . . and baskets . . . little chocolate candies . . . Easter candies . . . filled with vanilla and maple and cherry . . . in the front yard. Every Easter morning in the front yard . . . I'd hunt eggs and candies and baskets . . . nestled in the forsythia and the trunks of the maples in our front yard.

    I should have stayed out there tonight. I felt it. I knew I should have. But I just didn't feel like . . . my heart wasn't in it. Hard to do something when your heart ain't in it. I got this wig, thought it might perk me up a little . . . made this dress. Nice dress, I like it . . . soft and feminine. Don't misunderstand. I wasn't having to buy my drinks . . . I don't have to buy my drinks . . . but my heart wasn't in it. I just knew how it was going to end up . . . not the detail, but the total or something . . . and I got kind of queasy-stomached over that . . . cause I don't want to give up hope . . . and it's not that I have . . . sometimes you can just burn yourself . . . fry yourself . . . and you need to regenerate . . . juvinate . . . I don't know.

    One Easter morning, at nine or ten — my age, not the time — I awoke early, and I looked out the window . . . the living room window . . . and out on the lawn I saw them . . . hiding the eggs and candies and the basket in the early morning dew in the forsythia . . . and daffodils . . .

and I realized that the Easter bunny was just like Santa Claus. No different. I figured the other one out quicker . . . and I felt ashamed. I felt awful for them. There they were in the early morning hiding all those things, and I knew. I went back to bed, and when it came time for me to awaken . . . I pretended to be asleep, and I went through all the motions. For two years I did that . . . I know it was pretending, but it was all so much fun for all of us.

Tonight it wasn't no fun pretending. Least with the other, there were candies and eggs and baskets . . . but I wasn't getting nothing from this. So I came back . . . stopped at Cajun Bill's and picked you up some food and came back . . .

(Singing.) "Billy, don't be a hero, don't be a fool with your life. Billy don't be a hero, come back and make me your wife." Seventeen. He went off to the war in Vietnam, and I was faithful. And I sang that song, although I was already married to him . . . but he didn't die. He came back. But it wasn't the same . . . course we'd only been married for a few days before he left, so I don't guess I knew what being with him was . . . but I thought I knew . . . dreamt what it'd be . . . and then there was this evening in late October — no, late September — that he said, "It ain't working," and I said, "No, it ain't." And that I was sorry, but I didn't know what to do, and so tell me, and I'll try. But I didn't know what to do, and he said, "Don't worry." Next morning, he left. Just left. That was best, really the best, because why not? I mean, what's the point of hanging around when it's not working? Even if you still care, what's the point?

I worked the number up. I sing it sometimes. "Billy, don't be a hero." Some of the older ones like it. Some of the ones opposed to war, they like it. *(Softly she sings, then she stands, and performs the first part of the number with total concentration, as if on a stage.)*

(Realizing what she's done.) So I worked the bars. No sense sitting around thinking . . . crying over spilt . . . worked the bars as a singer. Mostly I guess . . . not only . . . not as . . . but as someone who's trying to find . . . I always sang when I was a kid . . . finally, I met someone . . . yes, finally. Six foot tall . . . drove a yellow Volkswagen bug . . . our first time was on the hood of that Volkswagen bug down on the Suwanee River. He got a divorce, and we got married, and then he got a divorce and got married again. Have you ever thought about how odd it is that Easter bunnies lay eggs? Before I knew that it was all something invented, I al-

ways wondered about that. Rabbits don't lay eggs, they have . . . they have babies. They're mammals, not birds. But the Easter bunny lays eggs, he doesn't or she doesn't — and that's another thing. How can he be a he and lay eggs — *she*s lay, not hes. That's really confusing if you think about it.

Then the last. He was the one that was so sweet, and . . . no one would have even believed it . . . Everyone thought he was so . . . and if anyone knew . . . they'd have assumed it was me . . . that I'd been fooling around . . . or that I'd done something . . . 'cause that nice, gentle man . . . wouldn't . . . but he did . . . he beat me . . . and I was a . . . I should have gotten out . . . but, well, I'd already lost twice, and the third — that would be really . . . three times and can't make a go of . . . so I figured I should try and do better . . . not to make him angry . . . 'cause when he was sweet, afterwards, he always was so sweet. But then it'd be a week or month or so . . . and I shouldn't have . . . 'cause when you let that happen . . . it's like an animal . . . dog . . . that gets beaten . . . beat a dog . . . enough and if it stays . . . don't run off . . . you snap your fingers and it's flat on . . . its stomach . . . tail between its legs . . . shaking . . . it's the way it works . . . and when he left . . . it took some time . . . and then I started getting angry . . . angry . . . just angry . . . at everything . . . angry at everyone . . . tonight . . . there I was angry . . . I saw the . . . knew them . . . knew how they . . . thought . . . didn't know . . . but thought . . . and I was so angry . . . and I thought of you kids . . . of Blue and Lydia . . . thought they're nice folks . . . they don't make me angry . . . when you moved in, I watched you and I thought, "Them's nice people . . . they're nice . . . it'd be wonderful if you could make friends with them . . . someone would just let you be" . . . and I could tell you don't have much . . . and I thought, "Maybe I can help them just a little" . . . I got quite a lot from the last . . . we had a joint checking, and I withdrew when he left . . . and I thought, "I can help them out" . . . I'm not rich . . . maybe it's something like a mother's feeling . . . I probably won't ever, probably never have a child. Not that I couldn't still, but I can't hold. I miscarry. No matter if I just lie in bed, I miscarry. That's why Bill and I got married, but I lost the child just after he left.

There was some strange Easter egg — maybe you had one, too, when you were a child. Mother can't remember where she got it. She thinks I dreamt it all. But it was different. First it'd seem like any of the others, covered with chocolate, but just inside the chocolate was a robin's egg blue sugar shell and rich caramel, more like toffee, and then a white shell and inside the cream was a green shell which held a snow white almond. Each Easter, I couldn't wait until I found this egg. I loved them so much. And they were always hidden in the most difficult places. Not only did they have all these colors, but they had the most intricate, highly complex designs. When I learned the order of color, I'd always look carefully when I was opening the various shells to see if something had been changed, that pink was in the place of blue, or that yellow had been substituted. It never was, but I was always curious to see, to look for a change, some sort of variation on the pattern.

It was awful over there. In that war. It must have been awful. Really terrible, but I can't understand why Billy changed so much.

The meal's cold by now, all cold, but would you like something to eat?

And The Winner Is . . .
David-Matthew Barnes

Scene: Backstage at the Academy Awards, during a commercial break.
Serio-Comic
Tracy Morrison (thirties), an African-American nominee for Best Actress.

When Tracy is egregiously 'dissed by her sister nominees during a live interview show at the Oscars, she lets loose with some very plain talk that manages to shut everyone up.

TRACY: Listen up, you little star *fuckers!* My name is Tracy Morrison and I'm here because I was nominated for my performance in "Sorry Is My Sister." Now, if y'all wanna be *nasty* about this, then I can be nasty. First of all, April Newton — everyone that I know has slept with your husband at least a dozen times — and they all complain about the same damn thing — two inches don't go very far in *my* neighborhood, *okay*?! And Pauline Emerson why don't you take your skinny white ass back to England and choke yourself on a pot of piss and tea. Your movies are almost as bad as your nose job — and don't even let me get started on how many sexually transmitted diseases you be spreadin' 'round town, you triflin' ho! You lay on a doorstep faster than the mornin' newspaper. And Rachel Riley — for some God-awful reason, some dumb ass put you in a movie and told you that you can act. *Shhh-eeeit.* That son of a bitch *lied* to your stupid ass and because of that — we all have to suffer by seeing your ugly grin smilin' up at us every time we go to Blockbuster. I could make one of your movies with ten dollars and a hooker from Harlem. And Danielle Taylor — you little drunk bitch — that sweet innocent routine doesn't fool *me.* You've got an arrest record a mile long and more ex-boyfriends than Elizabeth Taylor. In a year, you'll be burned out, used up and doing infomercials. I, myself, worked three jobs trying to put myself through college. I've studied every aspect of actin' you can possibly imagine. I've played every maid, call girl and the wife of countless dope dealers — on every stage from here to Kentucky. It took me eleven years to get a part in a film — and now that I'm here — I'm not going anywhere! I got an agent. I got a manager. I got a lawyer. I got a publicist. I've got a per-

sonal *mothah fuckin'* assistant. And it's about time. I deserve all this —
because unlike the four of you *dirty tramps* — I live an *honest* life with
dignity and self-respect. I *care* about the movies I make and not the size
of my bank account. So if the four of you can not maintain yourselves
like the decent young women God intended y'all to be, then step aside,
because I *can* and I *will*. It's not about box office. It's not about power.
It's not about having your face on every trashy magazine in America. It's
about givin' somethin' to the world — and believe you me, I'z got plenty
to give. Now, get that camera rollin', because I am ready for my interview.

Anton In Show Business

Jane Martin

Scene: A bare stage
Serio-Comic
T-Anne (twenty to forty), a stage manager.

>*Here, savvy T-Anne offers a sadly accurate description of the current state of American theatre as she prepares to organize auditions for a new production.*

T-ANNE: The American theater's in a shitload of trouble. *(Flash, crash.)* That's why the stage is bare, and it's a cast of six, one non-union. *(Flash, crash.)* I'm T-Anne, the stage manager, but I'm also in the play. *(Flash.)* Like a lot of plays you've seen at the end of the 20th century, we all have to play a lot of parts to make the whole thing economically viable . . . *(Crash.)* . . . HOMAGE TO THORNTON WILDER. *(Flash, crash. She drops the cloak. She wears blue jeans, a T-shirt, many keys at her belt.)* The date is *(Current date.),* 2000, just before noon. Well, I'll show you a little bit about how our profession is laid out. Up around here are the Broadway theaters, sort of between 42nd and 52nd Street, we like to think that's the heart of everything. City of New York, State of New York, United States of America, the world, the galaxy, the universe. Down over here is Greenwich Village, around there we do off-Broadway, that's good too. Now Tribeca, Soho, Lower East Side, we call that the "downtown scene," off-off stuff. An incredibly colorful group of people who despise realism and have all won the Obie Award . . . that's good too. Beyond that, radiating out in all directions for thousands of miles is something called "regional theater," which I understand once showed a lot of promise but has since degenerated into dying medieval fiefdoms and arrogant baronies producing small-cast comedies, cabaret musicals, mean-spirited new plays, and the occasional deconstructed classic, which everybody hates. After that, moving west, we reach the burning, uninhabitable desert and its militias who don't go to plays, and beyond that, singing a siren call, the twin evil kingdoms of Flick and Tube, the bourne from which no traveler returns. Now back to New York, thank God. Let's see, the Empire State Building, the Statue of Liberty and the Actors' Equity offices . . . that's our union. They make sure no more than 80 percent of our membership is out of work on any given day. And over there . . . yes, right over there is where we worship, yes sir, *The New York Times*. Well, that's about it. Now, with a short subway ride we get to one of the audition studios where producers and theaters come to find actors for their plays. Here's the front door, elevator up to the fifth floor, Studio C, where the San Antonio, Texas Actors Express has come to the big city to cast *The Three Sisters* by Anton Chekhov. He's Russian. At noon, you can always hear the actors doing their vocal warm-ups.

(Vocal warm-ups can be heard.)

Aya — there they are. Not much happens before noon. Theatre folks sleep late. So, another day's begun. There's Lisabette Cartwright walking into Studio C. She graduated from S.M.U. *(Southern Methodist)* drama department and began teaching third grade. Then she was invited all the way to New York for an audition because the producer once had her appendix removed by one of her uncles. Lisabettes' really excited, and her mom, who is at this moment canning okra, is too. Over there is Casey Mulgraw, the one dressed in the skirt/pants thing, a lot of people call her the Queen of off-off Broadway. She's a little hung over because she just celebrated the opening of her 200th play without ever having been paid a salary. She also has a yeast infection that is really pissing her off. In our town, we like to know the facts about everybody.

Anton In Show Business

Jane Martin

Scene: A bare stage
Serio-Comic
Lisabette (twenties), an idealistic young actress.

Following her first performing experience in New York, Lisabette here confirms her love of acting while expressing some hope for the future of theatre.

LISABETTE: 'Night. (*Lisabette remains in a single light. She looks around her.*) Wow. Crazy. It's so stupid, but I love to act. It always feels like anything could happen. That something wonderful could happen. It's just people, you know, just people doing it and watching it, but I think everybody hopes that it might turn out to be something more than that. Like people buy a ticket to the lottery, only this has more . . . heart to it. And most times, it doesn't turn out any better than the lottery, but sometimes . . . my dad runs a community center, and back in the day they did this play called *Raisin in the Sun*, just about a black family or something, and it was just people doing it. He said there was a grocery guy and a car mechanic, a waitress, but the whole thing had like . . . I don't know . . . aura, and people wanted to be there . . . so much that when they would practice at night, 'cause everybody had jobs, they had to open the doors at the center and hundreds of black people would just show up, show up for the play practice. They brought kids, they brought dinner, old people in wheelchairs, and they would hang around the whole time, kids running up and down, until the actors went home, night after night at practice, and when they finished, these people would stick around and they would line up outside like a . . . reception line . . . like a wedding . . . and the actors would walk down that line . . . "How you doin'? How you doin'?" shaking hands, pattin' on the kids, and the people would give them pies and yard flowers, and then the audience and the actors would all walk out, in the pitch dark, to the parking lot together. Nobody knew exactly what it was or why it happened. Some day I'd like to be in a play like that. I would. So I guess I'll go on . . . keep trying . . . what do you think? Could happen. Maybe. Maybe not. (*She looks at the audience.*) Well you came tonight anyway.
(*Blackout.*)

Apartment 3A
Jeff Daniels

Scene: An apartment in a mid-western city
Serio-Comic
Annie (thirties), a woman struggling to recover from a failed relationship while
at the same time being presented with the possibility of new love.

*Here, Annie describes the emotionally gruesome events that led to the end of
her relationship with Richard.*

ANNIE: I came home. I was early. And there he was. Or there should I say was
his bare ass because that's all I could see. That and her legs wrapped around
his back. Actually, they were way up around his neck. And I remember
thinking, what's Richard doing fucking a gymnast on top of my grandmother's dining room table. I actually stood there, marveling at their flex-
ibility. Mary Lou saw me first. Oh, my God, Richard. Richard. He turns.
He sees. Lots of silence. Lots of fumbling for clothing no one can find.
He tries to apologize. He tries to make it my fault. He tries to get me to
slap him. Hit him. Hate him. All I want to do is check the condition of
my grandmother's table. She leaves. I go into the kitchen. I come back
out with some furniture polish and I make what I thought was the love
of my fucking life polish that table until it shines. The next morning, I
put it out on the street and it's gone in thirty minutes. As is he. Cross
fade. Two weeks later. I'm in the corner market, Richard walks in. With
her. I say, Richard. He says, Annie. I say, what are you doing here. He
says, picking up a few things. I can't resist. "You mean, besides her?" She
calls me a bitch. Heads turn. The kid behind the counter looks up. I turn
to Richard and say, why. All I want is a reason why. And he looks at me
and he says . . . he says, because you care too much in a world that doesn't
give a shit anymore . . . and I stand there, in the middle of that market
and for the first time in my life, I can't think of a thing to say. So I run.
Out of my market. Out of my neighborhood. Out of my life as I know
it. I end up at the local U-Haul outlet where I rent a truck for the first
time in my life, pack up everything I own and start driving around the
city in circles until I come upon this sign. Apartment for Rent. Which I
do. After being told how lucky I am.

Asylum

Kara Hartzler

Scene: An office in the Department of Immigration and Naturalization Services.

Dramatic

Leah (twenties to thirties), an idealistic young woman trying to make a difference.

Leah's job is to interview individuals applying to the United States for political asylum. After a particularly frustrating day, she is asked why she does this for a living. She makes the following reply.

LEAH: Fine. This is why I came here.
(All of her barriers have broken down.)
I came here because I care about people, and I'm interested in human rights. I also came here because I wanted something that would look good on a resumé. I came here because I felt guilty when I read *Newsweek*. And I came here because I wanted to have a purpose.

[DANIEL: Anything else?]

LEAH: Sometimes when I've listened to three straight hours of hideous stories, this sick, jaded part of me starts to find them fascinating. I'll sit and think, "Wow, hung upside down and beaten with ice, I've never heard that one before." Then I'll file it away, in my mind, to recount to my father and my peacenik friends, and anyone who doubts that I'm a caring, compassionate person.

Back Story
"Maid of Athens"
David Rambo

Scene: Here and now

Dramatic

Ainsley (nineteen), a young woman struggling to keep it together in a family wounded by deconstruction.

> *Ainsley has cut her finger while helping to prepare a meal. Here, she recalls a special memory from her childhood in an effort to make the pain go away.*

AINSLEY: Shit! Oh . . . shit!

(She runs in wrapping a finger in a bloody swath of paper towel. It really hurts. She calls off.)

I'm okay. I've got an ice cube on it. Aunt Lou, put the potatoes in a pot of cold water. Except the one I got blood on.

(To herself, raising her bloodied fist, and taking deep breaths.)

Hold it above the heart. Come in, ice cube. Make it numb. Ice. Iceberg. Glacier. A big Alaskan glacier . . . on my finger. Kissing my finger, making the pain go away. Glaciers. Snow, in soft white drifts, like waves of icing on a wedding cake, like . . .

. . . Leonard Bernstein's hair. The summer I was eleven, and Reuben took me to Tanglewood. They remembered him, all the older musicians did, from when he played there. First clarinet. Reuben told them he was just teaching now and I was his star pupil. But they knew. It was a hot day, and when a drinker sweats, you can just smell it on them. We all could. And then, this . . . this wave of energy comes at us, and it's Leonard Bernstein. "Reuben! Reuben, God, where the hell have you been? Reuben, dear, darling, Reuben." And Leonard Bernstein's hugging Reuben and kissing him. Kissing! Then, Reuben says, "Lenny" — to Leonard Bernstein! — he says, "Lenny, this is Ainsley Belcher, my star pupil. She plays the clarinet." And then . . .

(She lowers the wounded hand, as if it's being held by Leonard Bernstein.)

Leonard Bernstein kisses my hand! Can't look him in the eye, or I'll sink like the Titanic. So I'm looking at his hair, these waves of thick, soft, white hair. Like snow. Big, soft, Alaskan glaciers.

They call rehearsal, and "Lenny" looks up at me, and quotes Lord Byron, my favorite poet!

"Maid of Athens, ere we part,

Give, oh give me back my heart."

And he left. For three hours I sat on the grass watching rehearsal, and didn't move a muscle or even go to the bathroom, even when the orchestra took a break. I didn't move.

(She hums a passage from Beethoven's Ode to Joy, *"conducting" with the wounded hand.)*

After that, when I practiced up in the cake room, if my cheeks hurt, or the muscles in my jaw got tired, I couldn't feel it. Leonard Bernstein was there. Conducting. Kissing my . . .

(Her hand.)

It doesn't hurt anymore.

Bad Party

Alison Diane Meehan

Scene: Here and now

Serio-Comic

Ashley (eighteen to twenty-five), a young woman describing a frustrating
and failed relationship.

*Here, Ashley recounts the strange direction her life took after meeting a guy
at a bad party.*

ASHLEY: It starts at a bad party. You talk to a guy about how lame the party
is; how much you hate school or how you can't believe your friends are
flirting with those guys. The next week at a slightly better party and you
aren't as drunk you start talking to the same guy. As you talk to him you
realize you're telling him more than you ever meant to. Suddenly, you
start seeing this guy everywhere. He knows everything about you. He
knows your friends, your family, where you work . . . he even knows what
you're thinking. This should scare you, but it doesn't. So you end up going
out with him a couple of times. Three months later you realize how much
trouble you're in. That's when you realize that you should ask him what
his name is. A year later you still haven't asked his name. You don't want
to hurt him. Then you're at Thanksgiving dinner and you want to in-
troduce him to your family, but you don't know his name so you just act
rude. In the middle of dinner he mentions to your mother how nice you'll
look in his grandmother's wedding dress and you finally start screaming.
"Married? You want to get married?? I don't even know your name!!" You
yell this over and over until you faint. Eventually you end up at the shrink's
talking about your ex-boyfriend and dying for a cigarette. When the good
doctor asks what your ex's name is you just smile. Then time is up and
you go outside and are about to light up that cigarette when you see this
guy who knows everything about your life walking by. And no, I never
did find out his name.

Be My Baby!
Michele Forsten

Scene: Here and now
Serio-Comic
Susie (thirties), a woman whose relationship has reached an impasse.

> *Susie and Clair have been happy and comfortable in their relationship for quite some time. When Clair indicates her desire to either have a baby of her own or to adopt, Susie realizes that she would rather spend the time and energy required to raise a child on herself. Here, she describes her feelings.*

SUSIE: I have some time to kill because Clair just called to say she'd be late coming home. Clair's so into her work. She doesn't make a whole lot of time to spend with me, her devoted spouse. I work a lot less and earn more. But money has never been Clair's thing and that's what attracted me to her in the first place. She has a good heart. I often lose sight of this, though, because she's always broke and it drives me crazy. I come from a family that measures success by how much money you have. My older sister Renee would bring home all these slimeball guys.
  (Slide of Renee, with a guy who looks like a gangster.)
  Quicker than you can say *gelt,* my grandma would get a handle on the guy's net worth. Like this:
  (Imitates her grandma, taking on Yiddish accent.)
  "Pleased to meet you . . . What do you do in business? . . . For a living you're a hit man? *Vos iz dus?* You mean you play baseball? . . . Oh, I see, you've made a killing . . . More than one . . . uh huh. Very impressive, a regular tycoon on Wall Street . . . Oh, you're not in the financial markets . . . Oh, the cement business. Well, whatever you do, you're a young man with a future. Have a good time, you two."
  (Squeezes out mop.)
  Okay, Okay. I exaggerate a little. But you get the idea. The need for financial security is genetically passed down in my family. Being in the closet for about a decade, I didn't have to put up with my dates getting the third degree, like my sister did.
  (Slide of hand waving outside almost closed closet door.)

I didn't bring anyone home. I would just get something like this:
(Imitates her grandma.)
"You know, you wouldn't have to work so hard if you had a husband.
(Slide of Susie with cutouts of a nuclear family.)
You're a nice looking girl. I don't know why you're not popular"
After one too many times of hearing this spiel I lost it and said,
"Grandma, I am popular . . .
(Slides of Susie with different girlfriends.)
. . . with the ladies. I'm a lesbian, bubbie, a dyke, a female feygaluh
. . . get it?"

She didn't answer and I walked away She never mentioned dating again. And I didn't mention my girlfriends. But you know the expression, "Silence equals death"? It took years for me to realize that grandma's silence was worse than her dating spiel. She was the most important person in my life, and she didn't accept me. Didn't accept *me.*

But I digress . . . Wait a minute. I never use the word *digress.* I guess I'm nervous talking in front of a group. I was always super quiet in school, never had any desire to be a teacher . . . Another way that Clair and I are different. She's a college professor. I'm picking up some of her vocabulary, though.

I'm getting off the fucking subject, that's what I'm doing. The subject of me and Clair. A lot of our lesbian friends, both single and couples, have kids now. Or they're planning for one. Clair gets depressed when she hears about this one adopting, that one being pregnant. I feel the time and energy a kid demands is better spent on myself. I have room to be a good partner, friend, co-worker, but not a good parent. I know that and just about accept it, almost.

It's funny, though. With so many friends and acquaintances having or getting kids, I'm feeling out of the loop. Like how I felt when I wasn't bringing boyfriends home. And just like back then, I start blaming myself. And that makes me mad, so angry that I want to scream at Claire, "Get used to it, I'm not going to change." But I don't. That attitude is so rigid it frightens me. I don't want to be like that.

Something's got to give. Clair and I argue too much. Sometimes from the second we get up. No, I'm not kidding. What? You think I'm exaggerating again? Being melodramatic to make a point? I beg your pardon.

Betty's Summer Vacation
Christopher Durang

Scene: A beach house
Serio-Comic
Mrs. Siezmagraff (forties to fifties), bombastic, loquacious and a tad naive.

Mrs. Siezmagraff has encountered Mr. Vanislaw, a derelict flasher in a women's changing room at the beach. She has brought him back to her vacation home, which she is currently sharing with her estranged daughter and several other unusual characters, including hapless Betty, who only wanted to enjoy a holiday by the sea. Here, Mrs. Siezmagraff prepares to go out on a date with the nearly feral peeping tom while chatting idly with Betty.

MRS. SIEZMAGRAFF: *(To Betty.)* I have these enormous red welts on my upper thighs. It's really unfortunate. I guess if I have sexual relations with Mr. Vanislaw, we better keep the lights off. Or he could be blindfolded, I guess. I've never done that, but people find it exciting, I'm told.
(Checking what Betty is cooking; or nibbling on something.)
I once saw this movie about a sorority hazing, and they showed these freshman girls this bowl of wiggling worms, then they blindfolded them and fed them what they assumed was the worms, but it was really just spaghetti, but the girls didn't know that and they choked and vomited and just had a terrible time.

[BETTY: A sorority hazing. How unusual.]

MRS. SIEZMAGRAFF: Yeah, I guess so. I have no idea what the movie was. I think that was the only scene of it I saw. It seemed to be from the fifties. I think the difference between the innocence of then versus now is that now they'd just go ahead and feed them the worms and not bother about switching to spaghetti. Isn't that sad? I feel something's been lost. But, oh well, we have someone coming to dinner, so I shouldn't let my feelings plummet down to the cellar, should I? La dee dah, oh for the life of a swan. Is that the saying? Oh, for the life of a something.

Big Love
Charles L. Mee

Scene: A country at war
Dramatic
Thyona (twenties), a woman driven by the passion of her convictions.

Here, Thyona speaks with great fire about injustice in the world and the need to take responsibility to rectify social wrongs before allowing oneself the luxury of love.

THYONA: All this talk of love.
    You think I'm not capable of love, too?
    But in the real world,
    if there is no justice
    there can be no love
    because there can be no love
    that is not freely offered
    and it cannot be free
    unless every person has equal standing
    and so
    the first order of business is to make a just society.
    You wish there would be love and mercy and compassion
    But first comes justice,
    and if there is no justice
    then those who are being taken advantage of
    have every right
    to take their oppressors
    to take those who stand in their way
    and drive them across the fields
    like frightened horses
    to set fire to their houses
    to ruin everything that comes to hand
    to hurl their corpses into wells
    where once there were houses
    to leave rubble

smoldering woodpiles
to leave shattered stones,
empty streets,
and silence
no living thing
no bird, no animal
no dogs,
no children,
not one stone left standing on another,
rather a wilderness of stones
and see if finally then
a lesson has been learned.
Because there are times
when this is justified
there are times, though you may not like it,
when this is all that human beings may rightly do and to shrink from it
is to be less than human.

Big Love
Charles L. Mee

Scene: A country at war
Dramatic
Lydia (twenties), a young woman in love.

*Lydia has chosen love over loyalty. Here, she tries her best to explain her feel-
ings to her sisters.*

LYDIA: You know, everything you say may be right, Thyona,
    but I have to ask myself,
    if it is
    then why don't I feel good about it?
    I have to somehow go on my gut instincts
    because sometimes
    you can convince yourself in your mind
    about the rightness of a thing
    and you try to find fault with your reasoning
    but you can't
    because
    however you turn it over in your mind
    it comes out right
    and so you have to think:
    I'm just a completely unreasonable person
    I know it's right but I don't think it is
    or I think it's right but I know it isn't
    and you could end up thinking
    you're just a moron
    or an emotional person
    or some sort of deficient sort of thing
    but really there are some things
    when you want to know the truth of them
    you have to use your whole person
    you have to use not just your mind and your feelings
    but your neurons or your cells or whatever

your whole body
to make some decisions
because they are too complicated for just your mind
or even just your mind and feelings
they need to be considered in some larger way
and in the largest way of all
I know in my bones
that I have to go with my heart
or whatever it is
I have to go with my whole being
when it says I love him and he loves me
and nothing else matters
even if other things do matter even quite a lot
even if I'm doing this in the midst of everyone getting killed
I can't help myself
and I don't think I should.
Probably this is how people end up marrying Nazis
but I can't help it.

Big Potato
Arthur Laurents

Scene: Here and now
Dramatic
Nessa (sixty to eighty), a Holocaust survivor determined to seek vengeance.

Nessa and her husband, Itzhak, have vowed to punish those responsible for the horrors of the Holocaust who remain alive and untouched. Here, she tells her son of their decision to travel to South America in search of war criminals.

NESSA: I am afraid of nothing. You want the truth? Ninety-two, I am, darling, and the day you were circumsized was the day I got Social Security. There is nothing I am too old for! Fifty I could be when you were born and a miracle it wouldn't be. A miracle is the ability to do whatever you want and I have it, my darling. I escaped Auschwitz, I can escape Florida. How much cash is downstairs? Those tickets are going to be changed. By me. To South America we are going, me and that young man who is your father. We'll bring you a souvenir, Sonny: Colombian Red, Argentinian Green, Brazilian Gold.
(Taking a drag from the joint he is smoking.)
And for the world — Martin Bormann! Don't tell me he's dead because I know he isn't. And if he is, we'll get Mengele or Mueller. A big potato, darling! Even you will be proud! Page One! Everyone will see and this time, no one will forget — you in particular!

Big Potato
Arthur Laurents

Scene: Here and now
Dramatic
Nessa (sixty to eighty), a Holocaust survivor determined to seek vengeance.

When Nessa's plan is challenged by her son, she confronts him with his ignorance of the depth of her suffering in Auschwitz.

NESSA: You never grew up! You played soldier, you got a little hurt, instead of growing up, you grew *in.* I grew up, sweetheart! I grew up with dead bodies like a rush hour in the subway! I grew up in a graveyard — up, not in, *up!*

[SONNY: I did time in my graveyard, sweetheart. Of course, it was a foreign graveyard.]

NESSA: All graveyards are foreign, you turtle. But nothing in the whole of all history was like ours. Yours was like all the rest: you were supposed to live. We were supposed to die, smart-ass. They told me I was — a thing, only there to die.

Do *you* know humiliation? For years, a lifetime! Humiliation! A thing, good for nothing but to die. But I don't. He don't. A hundred pounds between us, but we survive! Heroes! For two minutes. As long as it took to burn a new synagogue. So again we run — here. And here, we pretend like we are normal. After all that! But didn't I look like a normal woman, darling boy? Didn't I behave like a normal woman? I had children. I open a beauty parlor, I sit on my sitter, quiet like everyone else. But again it starts: the Russians, the Arabs, the Frenchies. Not here? No? Where oil matters more than life? Where they put swastikas on motorcycles to prove they are big men? Where I am again the smart little Jew business woman? Again humiliation? Again die? I don't sit on my quiet sitter anymore! I don't forget and *they* must not be forgotten! It has to stop!

Big Potato
Arthur Laurents

Scene: Here and now
Dramatic
Nessa (sixty to eighty), a Holocaust survivor determined to seek vengeance.

Nessa and Itzak finally manage to capture someone they believe to be a "big potato"; their grown children insist that they allow the suspected Nazi to go free. Here, Nessa angrily confronts her offspring revealing her passionate need for justice.

NESSA: Oh, sit down and be quiet.
[ROCHELLE: I will not. *(But she does.)*]
NESSA: *(Quietly.)* I was not relieved when you left my house, Rochelle. You were. I was too much for you. I still am.

(To Sonny.)

Also for you. You think I haven't known what the both of you think of me? Your admiration is only that I still go on. I'm just a tiresome, mad old fool with an obsession. Yes! I *am* obsessed — with living, you idiots! That's what I learned from the camps: How glorious it is! That's what I want for him, for me, for you.

(A plea to Sonny.)

For you! . . . Not your fantasy of screwing your clients in the back room. Yes: fantasy! Oh, I play along, I encourage because that at least is a way to keep alive — if it is *real.* But your dreams are dry! *Real* life is what I tried to breathe into you. The both of you! With the blood pumping and the juices flowing and the heart screaming! But that is too much for you, too enormous! And what is your answer? "You're a bad momma. Shut up." How small. How tiny.

Blue Movie

Jay Boyer

Scene: A bedroom
Serio-Comic
Woman (thirties to forties).

When she retires for the evening, this unsuspecting wife discovers that her hubby has fallen asleep while watching a porn film. Here, she offers insight into her married life while watching the film.

The point of this monologue is that the speaker's response to the blue movie she finds on her television screen playing in silence at the foot of her bed is much more complex than what she says to her sleeping mate, and toward that end it is sparely written. Its intent is to give an actress a chance to show off her talent for physical comedy. Hence, where there are ellipses below, there should be on the stage changes in facial expression and posture and the like as she responds to what she sees. How broad this should be played is the choice of the actress. But it has been written so that what she says should follow from or counterpoint whatever physical business she brings to the script.
Lights up as the speaker comes to the bed sleepily, her hair tousled, her eyes half-shut. From the audience's perspective her spouse is already asleep beneath the covers, an effect that can be had for no more trouble than stuffing that side of the bed with pillows.

WOMAN: Why'd you let me fall asleep on the couch, are you still up? . . . What are you watching? . . . What in God's name . . . What *is* this you're watching? . . . Is this what's on cable at this time of the morning? . . . It's pretty explicit, isn't it . . . Tell me you're not serious . . . Oh — shoot me now . . . Oh NO. Look at that . . . What are those, Triple-E cup or something? . . . She's SO gross. She's . . . another woman would look at her and think, "That woman's a cow" . . . Watch what they're doing. I hope you're as bored with this as I am . . . The blonde one's not that gross, okay. But only by comparison. She's pretty gross though . . . When we met, why were all your girlfriends blonde? What is with blonde, some kind of purity-madonna-virgin-whore thing? . . . I'm just asking. What is it with men and blondes? . . . Not that any of yours were exactly pure. Once you have testosterone, what is with blonde, is all I want to know from you . . . I don't want to think about who you were sleeping with, had any of them even heard of hygiene, or what you might be passing along . . . Oh — that is so sick . . . What is it about men that makes them want to degrade a woman? . . . You're a man, no really, I'm asking, where's the allure? What pleasure is there in that for you people, how is that a turn-on? . . . Look. Are they kidding? Does all sex have to be twisted and sick? . . . Some pathetic male fantasy . . . Is that arousing to you people? . . . Who'd do that to themselves? They don't, look, they don't move when she, I could never . . . I hope they're not going to do what I think they're going to do . . . OH MY GOD . . . Do you suppose they write this out in advance? Can you imagine the script?! Ala *Citizen Kane* the camera cranes higher and higher until it happens upon a scene of completely per-verted sodomy . . . What did I tell you? They keep pointing straight up in the air . . . They're like a totally separate entity . . . Tupperware, or something . . . Oh God, Oh — now *there's* something I couldn't have lived without seeing. That is more about this woman than I really cared to know. Thank you for letting me watch; I'm a much better person now . . . How is she doing that with her legs? It looks like they've got five legs between them, HOW IS SHE DOING THAT WITH HER LEGS . . . When you're like, you know, twelve years old and you're going through puberty, is that who you're envisioning, is that how you think women look when they take off their clothes . . . This is exactly my point: an-other woman looks at a woman like that and thinks, Honey, something new, it's called hygiene . . . She looks like she ought to have a valve on her back. You know, open it and she ought to go flying around the room, shriveling into nothing, is how she looks . . . You'd like what they're doing now . . . Well I think — don't bother to deny it — I think you'd have to admit, you're a little conflicted, sexually, I mean. I think you'll have to admit that . . . Which explains why all the sports. And your first wife . . . I blame that on your mother. After what she did to your psyche, it's amaz-ing you can have sex at all . . . Oh God! That's totally gross . . . Oh my God THAT IS SO EROTIC, I'm telling you . . . Doesn't she have friends? What if she's shopping at Target, what if they saw? . . . What if she has children some day, and there it is for posterity? . . . Right. Nice touch. Like we need to see her tongue to get it . . . Is that a stimulating view, is it just me? . . . Men are slime. This is totally lame male fantasy, isn't it. Men are categorically a lower form of life. Completely off the food chain . . . That was so. Not. Sensual . . . Okay, okay . . . What they're doing now isn't so bad — It's not *as-bad* maybe. It's still bad though, it's just not as homicidally aggressive toward women . . . All right, if you're a man — if you're on a desert island — if you're a registered sex offender, who knows, this is — I admit it, this is sort of erotic . . . That much, I'll give you. Sick — but erotic . . . He seems to like her, doesn't he. He should register that thing with his local police . . . You should watch this, hey, you don't want to miss, are you watching this — it's your ripe little blonde. But that's not her real hair. They're extensions.

Claudia Lazlo

Arthur Laurents

Scene: A theater
Serio-Comic
Madeline (forties), a grand dame of the stage.

Madeline is in rehearsals for "Claudia Lazlo," the role of her career. When she is late for scene work, her director asks her what kept her. Here, the great actress makes the following reply.

MADELINE: I was on the phone, darling. On the phone? Yes, on the phone, long distance. With my lover? With my agent? I have neither. With my son, Moses. Who was in tears. Do you know the sound of an adolescent boy in tears? It's awful. I never want to hear it again . . . His headmaster at Ridgefield — not one of the grandest of prep schools, no, they wouldn't take him. Not because of him — he's brilliant and gorgeous and terrified. No, because of me: actress; single mother. Neither divorced nor separated.
(Imitating a grand headmaster.)
"No father, Mrs. Gray?"
"I call you — ah ha — Mrs. Gray because the mothers of all our boys who come to us are — ah ha — Mrs. But no father at all, Mrs. Gray?"
(As herself.)
"No, Reverend, no daddy at all. I found him in the bull rushes. Why did you think I called him Moses?" . . . When I was seven months gone and showing big, I went home to Albuquerque. He isn't big now, my boy. Well formed, great legs but not big. I was and proud to be, so I went home where I hadn't been in almost 20 years. The esteemed professor who is also my daddy didn't even say Hello. Just pointed to my belly and said: "If it's a boy, bring him around." Tightened his Paisley bow tie, then turned and went back into the house I had run away from . . . The headmaster at Ridgefield also favors bow ties. I should have taken that into consideration before turning Moses over to him. This morning, he summoned the boy to inform him his mother's check for the semester had bounced. Perfectly true: it had. Burn me at the stake, put me in stocks, flog me —

the check bounced and not just yesterday. We have discussed it 10, 12, days ago — maybe 2, 3 weeks ago. I could see over the phone he was wearing a polka-dot bow tie. I had assured him but to no avail, darling. He ordered Moses to call me *now!* The boy did. Through his tears, he begged me to get a tuition check to the headmaster fast — *now!* "And be sure it doesn't bounce, Mom." The prick meant to humiliate me, of course. He doesn't care it was my kid he humiliated. How can they allow some-one like that to be in charge of children? Do you wonder the boy was in tears? . . . Well, it took a very long time to calm him down. That's why I was "so very late."

Coaster
Adam Langer

Scene: Chicago
Serio-Comic
Carri (twenties), a dancer.

> *Here, this free-spirit describes her philosophy of life, revealing a mind that is as direct as it is bold.*

CARRI: I don't believe in hypochondria. I don't believe in the word. I believe that there are things out there that you can't see that are just as deadly as all the microorganisms and all the germs and all the bacteria that people say they can see. I believe you can be flattened just as bad by a gust of bad energy as you can get flattened by a Dodge Truck. I believe that bad people are just as contagious as germs, and their moods are worse. I believe the right person's hand on your ass can do just as much good as a bottle full of St. Joseph's orange-flavored chewable aspirin for adults. That's just what I believe. I believe all the world's truths, such as they are, can be found in song lyrics. And not just in good ones, the bad ones most of all, like "Love the One You're With," "Why Don't We Do It In The Road?" and "You Gotta Stand For Somethin' Or You'll Fall For Anything." I believe the smallest things in life should make a person happy — the smell of a rose, the yawn of a Labrador puppy, rain falling on a spring day. So why the hell am I so depressed all the time? I don't know. People tell me all the time I should become an actress, that I've really got a knack for it, but I wouldn't know how to do that. I don't know how you can make a part of yourself not real. I'm a very spiritual person. I know I was here before and I was a much happier person then. I know I was here before that and I was a much sadder person then. I believe drugs are natural as water and both can cure you and both can kill you. I think of all the evil things in the world, the worst thing of all of them is a liar, but I believe that even the biggest liars in the world think on some level they're telling the truth. I believe anyone who says they don't believe in God is lying to herself. And the same goes for anyone who says they do. I believe every word ever invented in any language is a little kind of lie.

I believe truth only exists in movement. I believe truth exists only in action and everything else is a lie. There was one night when the moonlight was shining in through the blinds and I watched my shadow on the floor of the studio sliced into pieces by the blinds, and as I moved, I was transfixed by the image of my body moving on the floor and as I watched the broken shadow, I realized at that moment that everything it was doing was right and everything I was doing was wrong. You could say that the two were the same, but if you said that, all that would mean is you didn't understand what I just said. All opinions are shit. That's why I work in the restaurant. It helps pay the bills.

Coaster
Adam Langer

Scene: Chicago
Serio-Comic
Carri (twenties), a dancer.

> *When Carri meets Sam, she is trying to choreograph a dance recital based on diseases of the body, and he is convinced that he's dying of a brain tumor, so naturally they hit it off. Following a casual date at a Def Leppard concert, Carri saves them both a bit of awkwardness by speaking frankly about their prospects of spending the night together.*

CARRI: I wish people would always be that direct, say what's on their minds.

[SAM: Being honest is just being self-serving. Self-serving and self-righteous.]

CARRI: That's fucked up.

[SAM: A person can afford a form of protocol.]

CARRI: That's just bullshit, because everyone knows when you're lying. It's just too much trouble to call you on it. Forms of protocol — what that means — you're gonna lie. I know you're gonna lie. You lie. You know I know that you're lying, but what we agree — our form of protocol — is that I'm not going to call you on it. I'm just gonna sit here with this little bullshit smile on, so this shit is not *addressed*. Fuck that. Like us. Sitting here. You drinking an ice water, me eating an ice cream. I'm going to watch you drinking your water, you're gonna watch me eating my ice cream. I'm gonna talk about this, you're gonna talk about that. I'm gonna talk about my dance, how fucked up it's going, how I think it's shit, and you're gonna go yeah yeah yeah yeah yeah and you're gonna talk about your symptoms — some tumor, some exaggerated headache, some whatever — and I'm gonna go yeah yeah yeah yeah yeah, all the while avoiding what's going on in your head and what's going on in mine, how you're gonna try to talk your way through this "my girlfriend's moving, our relationship's kinda bullshit" thing so we can wind up fucking or touching my tits or just making out or whatever, and how I'm thinking "Nah, nah. I'm not into that," so we talk about other stuff, because you kinda know already if it hasn't happened yet, then it's not going to happen and what's the point of finding that out for certain and how I'm having a good time just sitting here and I don't want to fuck it up by being a bitch — not that that makes me one — but why bother having you think that, 'cause you're an all right guy and who knows maybe if whatever these symptoms are don't turn out to be something horrible and sexually transmitted, I mean who knows? Keep your options open, I guess. But just fuck some guy for the hell of it? Maybe a couple of years ago when I was doing a lot of coke and my self-image was shit and you figure fuck this guy, maybe he'll stick around, I don't know — whatever bullshit I was thinking. But now, there's no net benefit and opportunity cost? That's basically nil, because what am I missing? When it comes down to it. 10 percent chance — something I'll remember fondly. 40 percent change — something I'll regret. 50 percent chance — something I'll have no opinion about whatsoever. I've got better things to do with my time. So, are you gonna come watch my recital next week?

[SAM: Sure.]

CARRI: There's beer.

False Hopes
David-Matthew Barnes

Scene: Here and now
Dramatic
Claudia (thirties), a woman who is angry with her sister.

Claudia's sister, Amy, has become pregnant from participating in an un-savory office affair. When Amy turns to Claudia — who cannot have children of her own — for help, she finds a less-than-sympathetic response.

CLAUDIA: What do you want from me, Amy? You want me to tell you that it's okay? You want me to make you feel better for having an affair with a man who *used* you? I won't do it! You're on your own. It was *your* decision to sleep with the man. It was *your* decision to resort to the only tactic you knew in order to advance your career. Now, you have to pay the price. Just like I have to pay the price. I'm *still* paying the price for *your* mistakes! This whole office is full of gossip about you. But guess what? *I'm* your sister and that makes me guilty by association. I'm the sister of the *whore* of this corporation and now she's gone and gotten her fool self knocked up. Don't ask me for support. Don't ask me for advice or help or forgiveness. You don't deserve it. The only thing you're concerned about is yourself and your career. Now, if you'll excuse me, I have to get back to work.

The Fish In The Dumpster

Nancy Gall-Clayton

Scene: Outside a SuperAmerica gas station off an expressway exit near a small
rural community.

Dramatic

Angie (sixteen to eighteen), a young homeless woman.

> *Angie has been deposited at the gas station by the truck driver she'd been trav-*
> *eling with until he discovered that she was pregnant. Here, she tells the tragic*
> *story of her pregnancy and subsequent disposal of her newborn child.*

ANGIE: It was a flip-floppy fish-sort-of-feeling, mostly right around my belly
button — strong sometimes, like one of them orange fishes flinging itself upstream on the nature shows you see on TV and all.

I thought I might be able to kill the thing if I drunk a whole bunch
of liquid — not alcohol, I don't care for the taste and I didn't want to
pickle it — but water so cold it would sting my teeth — and apple juice
and Kool-aid — healthy drinks, things they give kids in daycare, things
to shock it.

And if I couldn't kill it while it was *in* me, I planned to squeeze it
out by filling my belly with more food than I could hold, like how water
spills over the edge of the tub when you run it too long and you step in
and something has to give. I sure wish I could tell Jimmy it worked.

He was real nice, Jimmy. I wouldn't have stayed with him otherwise,
now would I? *Is* nice, I should say. Winter was coming when we met,
and he bought me a coat right off. It had one of them fake fur collars
that feel nice and deeplike and smooth up against your cheek.

Jimmy and me, we met by the Krispy Kreme doughnut case at a
Thornton's somewhere in Indiana. I was drinking coffee with lots of that
Amaretta flavoring in it. The one in the little purple container. Gee, I
could drink that stuff straight! Actually, I do sometimes.

Anyways, there I was, kinda leaning on the doughnut case, getting
ready to take a sip outa my coffee, and he walks in and smiles at me, like
he knows some secret, a good secret I mean, and he looks smack dab into
my eyes. Something — fate, I guess you might call it — makes me toast

him. I was kind of taken with his gold tooth with the heart cutout, too. I hold up my coffee cup and holler, "Cheers!" like we was old pals celebrating some important occasion, maybe a tenth wedding anniversary or something. He sees right off I have a little class, a little more knowledge than the usual lady you see at Thornton's.

"Hold that," he says and swats me on the bottom and walks off in the direction of the men's room. "Hold what?" I'm thinking to myself. "Hold what? The coffee? The way I'm standing? Something he meant to hand me?"

When he comes back out, he smiles again, and the sunlight kinda bounces off that gold heart on his tooth. He bumps his leg smack into mine — accidentally on purpose, you know. "You with someone?" he asks.

"You," I say, deciding on the spot. "You, if that's your 18-wheeler out there."

The night I met him I looked fine, *real* fine, but then I am the kind that flowers after midnight. My hair was tied back in a pony tail, white-blonde I think it was, and I had me an almost new pair of hiking boots with rawhide laces so long I had to wrap them 'round my ankles twice. My roomie at the shelter give 'em to me 'cause they pinched her toes.

Jimmy must have liked the way I looked 'cause soon as I said that, he said, "Come on," and away we went. He told me we were heading to Oklahoma with a load of bikes. Said he delivered them all over. Isn't that something? I didn't know kids rode bikes so much these days. Me, I was twelve the last time I was on a bike and racing like heck to get away from a mean dog that ended up sinking its teeth into my rear end. The sheriff comes out and said I should pull down my pants and let him take a look at the bite, but my dad run the guy off. I didn't get no rabies if that's what you're wondering.

Almost as soon as I get in the truck, Jimmy asks me if I have any dreams, so I know right off that he is a quality-type person. I decide to show him I'm one, too, and ask him to go first. His dream, I wasn't expecting nothing about truck driving now, but his dream is to drive cross-country in a truck carrying three layers of brand new cars. Three layers, like one of them wedding cakes rich people have. He wants to climb into the very highest car, smoke Marlboro's, and watch the sky some night when the stars are shooting around. Me, I ain't never seen shooting stars, but he did several times, he said. He got so caught up telling me 'bout it, he kinda forgot to ask what my dream is, and I never did tell him neither, and it's no never mind now. Really.

Jimmy had fixed up the back of his truck real nice with a mattress, three pillows, a big 'ole fluffy quilt he bought in Tennessee, and a wooden box to put things in. Glued on one end of the box is this picture of a tall, thin dancing lady wearing a hat of fruit, looking like a foreigner who could click her high heels and dance and sing all at the same time. Everything about her is stretched out somehow, like she's been one of those very tall, thin babies born with the long fingers that make everybody say, "Oh, she's going to be a piano player," even if no one in the family knows the difference between the white keys and the pedals. When I was in Vacation Bible School one time, I asked the minister why the song didn't get no faster when the lady playing pressed on the pedals, and I *do* know the difference. But I can't play. Never went back to that Vacation Bible School either, just that one summer when I stayed up to Gram's 'cause dad was off somewhere doing construction, and mom, she wrote herself a bad check or two and they took me away from her till she paid her debt to society.

Anyway, it was awful cozy snuggling with Jimmy in the back of that truck. I just loved it when he'd fling his long legs over me like he was trying to protect me from something evil. He couldn't, of course, because the evil thing was *in* me.

I think it was June when it began flipping around so fierce-like. In the trucking life, your days run together kinda like fence posts out here in Kansas and it just mighta been May or July, I can't say certain for sure. I couldn't keep up with the time of day neither 'cause my watch was missing the hour hand. Fell off for some reason. It's still in there though. See?

(Points.)

When you press down on both buttons, it makes a green glow. I like to pretend this green opens into a magic world where pixies live. I might still believe in pixies. But don't tell no one, okay?

Anyways, it was fall when Jimmy told me he didn't like fat women. Had to be fall 'cause school buses were suddenly everywhere. I was fat all right — my belly was almost full enough to flood the fish out, but to please him, I pretended to go on a diet. Jimmy musta knowed my heart wasn't in it though; elsewise, he never would have left me at this Super-America last week. He mighta been mad 'cause I spent too long in the ladies' room that night talking to the fish, but I really couldn't help it. When I finally come out, I got me a couple extra Amarettas and he says, "Come on, Angie. I'm gonna be late." I never did hear him worrying about being late 'fore that night. I shoulda knowed something was up.

I got in the truck and we was about to drive out of this here very parking lot when Jimmy stops real sudden-like and hands me a Ben Franklin. "Hon," he says, sounding kinda sweet and more like himself again, "Go in and get me some Marlboros."

"You know they won't take that this time of night," I says, trying real hard to think about the fruit-hat lady on the wooden box to take my mind off the fierce pains down in my belly.

"Here," he says, taking Ben back and handing me two twenties. Now that there should have been a big enough clue, him giving me *two* bills and all, but I wasn't thinking too clear at the time. When I come out with the Marlboros, the truck is gone. Just plain gone. I stare real hard in every direction and then I go walking down

(Pointing.)

that little road over there. Guess what's down there? A *Welfare Office.* I've been trying to puzzle out if Jimmy knew it was there, if he planned this, but I can't believe that, I really can't. Irregardless, I have no mind to talk to a social worker, leastwise not until first frost. I didn't have time to talk to one the night he drove off, that's certain for sure. That last sip of coffee musta done it. About the time I get back from my walk and go over to that pump,

(Pointing.)

no, that diesel pump, it was, trying to spot the 18-wheeler,

(Pointing in another direction.)

Gallons of liquid suddenly gush out from between my legs. That fish starts talking real loud and I'm listening real hard, too. The fish says go back in them woods behind the dumpster, back there up the hill a little.

(Points.)

And off I go. You'll never guess what I find by the dumpster — a long box with a picture of a shiny red bike on it! *And* a bike in it.

I lean the box against the dumpster and make myself a comfy, cozy, private space where nobody can bother me and where I can squat down and push out my fish. Kind of like a playhouse with two walls. I got the dumpster on one side, and the bike box on one side and the woods seems like it stretches out into forever behind me. Overhead, stars are twinkling down. The building looks real bright against the darkness, and I can hear cars and trucks whooshing by every so often while I'm a-grunting and a-groaning.

After a whole lot of commotion in my belly — I mean a whole lot! — that fish finally swims outa me and lands on a pile of wet leaves. It's slimy and slick when I try to pick it up, and its tail is still attached to something up inside me. I hack at the tail with a tin can lid I find on the ground and cut myself. Not a big cut — here see.

(Shows her cut.)

Anyway I'm noticing newspapers stacked up beside the dumpster. I tell myself I should wrap up the fish in a newspaper and I do. It flops around for a minute — *that* was no surprise — and even makes a little whimpering sound. I ignore everything and just fling the whole mess into the dumpster. "Good-bye, Amaretta," I say, "and good riddance." Probably shouldn't give it the name of something I like, but it was all I could think of at the time. It landed near a big 'ole mound of coffee grounds.

Then I pressed them buttons on my watch and thought about magic and pixies. I spread out the coat Jimmy got me at the Salvation Army, and I lay me down to sleep just like that prayer they say on TV.

That was only five days ago, I think, four or five. It was yesterday when a giant truck come along and backed up to the dumpster and carried it off. I guess the fish is in the landfill somewheres by now and can't bother nobody. Jimmy will be glad to know that, I 'spect. I'm figuring he'll be stopping off on his way back to Ohio. He wouldn't have left the bike or give me that money unless he was coming back, you know? He only left 'cause he was gonna be late for something.

And that's why I been sleeping in the woods and just coming in for snacks and the bathroom after midnight, like now. If I go off somewhere, he won't have no way to find me. Yeah, Jimmy, why he'll be back real soon, so, no, mister, thanks all the same, but I really can't go off with you.

(Pause.)

I don't mind talking a spell longer though. And oh! I just remembered: I've still got that pack of Marlboros I bought for Jimmy. They're down in this pocket next to my Amarettas. Would you like a smoke?

For Now
Jocelyn Beard

Scene: Here and now
Serio-Comic
Crimson (fifteen to seventeen), a young woman struggling with her sexual
   orientation.

Here, Crimson weighs her various options and prospects for the future.

CRIMSON: I'm trying to make up my mind about whether or not I should be
   gay. It's a big decision. I mean, I guess I am . . . gay . . . whatever that
   means. I don't feel very gay. I feel like shit. Girls . . . women . . . well,
   they get to me, you know? Being with a beautiful girl makes me feel the
   same way my friend, Robby, says he feels when he's with Krissi Eversole
   . . . in fact, when I'm standing next to Krissi Eversole in the gym lock-
   erroom I feel like my heart is going to bust right out of my chest. I can't
   explain it any better than that.
      But I have to consider what my mom calls my "prospects."
      Next year I'll graduate and if I'm lucky I'll go to one of the state col-
   leges. If I'm luckier still I just might learn something that will help me
   make money one day. How much is enough? I have no freaking idea. If
   all I want is a crappy little condo and a shit box Toyota to drive back and
   forth to work in, then I guess enough won't be too much . . . say, a computer programmer or accountant . . . something like that. But, that's not
   what I want. I want a beautiful old house in the country, six big dogs,
   horses, cats and . . . and . . . kids. I want kids. I can't help the way I feel
   about that any more than I can help the way I feel about Krissi Eversole.
      If I'm going to pay for that house in the country and everything else
   all by myself, then computer programmer just won't cut it.
      If I get married, on the other hand . . . you know, to a guy. A nice
   guy like Robby. If I get married to a guy, then my chances for the house,
   the dogs and the kids improve exponentially. If I get married to a guy,
   my chances for practically everything improve exponentially.
      If I decide to be gay I can kiss that house and the kids good-bye. If
   I decide to be gay I can kiss practically everything that I've ever hoped

for or dreamed about good-bye. If I decide to be gay then I have to stop being one of "us" and start being one of "them." Problem is: I like being one of "us." I like fitting in. I like being liked. I mean, I'm sure that there must be quite a few fledgling dykes here at Wonder Bread High, but no one — probably not even them — knows who they are. I don't want to be the first. That's not me.

I read about this girl who wanted to be the first girl to go to this famous all boys military academy so bad that getting there almost killed her. That is definitely not me. I like it right here in the middle where it's safe. No one looks at me. No one wonders about me. I'm just like everybody else. If I decide to be gay, all that's gonna change. Robby will stop being my best friend, no one will want to sit near me in the cafeteria or the library and Krissi Eversole will turn and run every time she sees me coming. I know that past all that, beyond the looks and the name-calling and loss of social stature is something incredibly good. Acceptance and self-love, maybe? Who knows? There's no one around to explain it to me. All I know is that I just can't see past all the bad stuff. For now. Maybe that will change.

So for now, I'm still in the middle. For now I'm still deciding whether or not I should be gay. I'm still Robby's best friend and my gym locker is still right next to Krissi's. When Robby and Krissi kiss I feel like I'm right there with them and it's not too bad. For now. Best of all, I get to keep my fantasy about the beautiful old house in the country for a little while longer. Of course in my fantasy, I share the house with the kids, the dogs and Krissi Eversole. We can wait until the economy picks up a little before we get the horses.

Fuddy Meers

David Lindsay-Abaire

Scene: Here and now
Dramatic
Claire (forties), a woman struggling with memory loss.

> *An injury has left Claire with no long-term memory. Every day she must re-learn everything she learned the day before. When she is brought to her mother's house by a mysterious man claiming to be her brother, she is visited by a sudden memory from her childhood.*

CLAIRE: You remember that dog? Skinny old thing Mr. Cuthart kept tied up in the front lawn all day? Daddy always said he was gonna report him. Remember she just sat in the sun, biting at her scabs? Cuthart didn't even give her any water.

[GERTIE: Who do teching bat?]

CLAIRE: Nancy. So I'd sneak down the road with my squirt gun, and spritz water into her mouth and she'd bark.

[GERTIE: Uh-huh. I bee rye bag. *(Rushes off to another part of the house.)*]

CLAIRE: And one day, when Cuthart was downtown, I untied her and let her run around a little. But she darted straight into the road, just as Daddy's pickup was coming around the curve, and he didn't see her, so he plowed into her. *(Calls off.)* Do you remember Daddy and I came through the back door, Mama? And Nancy was hanging out of his arms like a set of broken-up bagpipes. And he spread her out on the kitchen floor and she was breathing real hard. And the pain was humming off of her like I could hear it. And she just let the pain take her over. And that's all she was. This *pained* thing. *(Gertie enters with a cookie tin. Claire's story has brought her back into the room.)* And Daddy was bent over her, talking to her real quiet. And all of a sudden Nancy stood up, like it was a new day, and she started running around the kitchen like she wasn't half-dead, barking and clicking her nails against the floor tiles. And we were all shocked because Nancy was like a puppy all of a sudden, not that bony heap on the floor. She was this fireball for about three minutes, until she got tired again, and curled up beside the sink and went to sleep and died like it meant nothing. You remember how all that happened to her? It's funny how almost everything else is gone to me, and that sad old dog just came into my head.

Going To Bordeaux
Richard Lay

Scene: Bordeaux, France

Dramatic

Nell (forties to fifties), a woman who feels as though her family has deserted
    her.

> *Nell and Vincent have traveled to France to visit their daughter, Dana. When
> Nell finds out that Dana has a son and that she's a grandmother, she tries her
> best not to lose it.*

NELL: Is he a nice young man? I'm sure we'll like him when we get to know
    him. Daughters sometimes pick men who are like their fathers — I'm
    sure you didn't make that mistake. Is he American or a Frenchman you
    met at home? We'd like to meet his father and mother? You said in the
    postcard that he's a friend — does that mean you never married? Is your
    little boy christened? . . . We are not interfering . . . We just came to Bor-
    deaux because we are so pleased, so falling down pleased that our little
    girl is standing on her own two feet. Can you see what I'm saying. Can
    you see it from our point of view. *(Starts weeping.)* We just want to be
    normal grandparents. All my friends have grandchildren who live just
    around the corner. They pop in for coffee every day and take the little
    ones to the Mall . . . They don't have to wait five years for a postcard.
    Not that that is a criticism . . . By no means. You know what I mean
    Dana. It's just that I want us to be a normal family again . . . I want us
    to love each other and laugh and cry and have crisis and dream about
    each other . . . Not always nightmares.

Going To Bordeaux

Richard Lay

Scene: Bordeaux, France

Dramatic

Nell (forties to fifties), a woman who feels as though her family has deserted her.

Nell and Vincent are in for a bigger surprise than a grandson . . . Dana is gay and living with a woman. When Nell digests this tidbit, she surprises everyone with the following memory from her childhood.

NELL: *(Looking into space.)* I had a girlfriend once. In college. I also had a boyfriend but I was more interested in Jill. We used to lie in a cornfield after class with lemonade and cookies and just stroke each other's hair. We played a game. It was called Practicing How To Kiss Boys . . . and we would kiss each other and relate it to what might happen with our boyfriends after the Saturday dance. The kissing made me feel dizzy and I'd look up at the blue sky and it would be going round and round as if someone had cast a magic spell on me. Jill used to call me Juicy Lips and it gave me pleasure to hear her call me that. I haven't thought about her for years. She died in a car accident during our last semester and I used to put daffodils on her grave and blow her a kiss. So Dana and Charley, yeah, I understand strong feelings between women. What's wrong with it? . . . There's nothing wrong with it? Men don't like it because they are repressing their feminine side. They all have one, even you Vincent . . . Remember when I caught you wearing my lipstick when you were doing a self-portrait.

Holy Mothers
(Die Präsidentinnen)
Werner Schwab
Translated by Meredith Oakes

Scene: A small kitchen/living room
Dramatic
Grete (fifties to sixties), pensioner, quite fat, beehive hairstyle, tastelessly
dressed, lots of cheap jewelry, heavy makeup.

*When a friend suggests that Grete's life has been more fun than most, this un-
happy woman hastens to correct her misconception.*

GRETE: *(Furious.)* Don't you think you're being rather nasty? How can you be
so nasty behind that laughing face of yours? Do you think my life has all
been one big barrel of laughs? First I was divorced, then I was widowed.
Do you think marriage is one great big pleasure trip? What about Kurti,
my first husband? And Hannelore? What do you imagine it's like when
you know, because you can't help knowing, that your very own husband
is punishing your very own daughter in your very own bed? What about
that, for God's sake?

What you do is, you wait and see, you wait and see what providence
has in mind for people. But you have to give providence the space to work,
until you finally find out what it's going to be. And at last, when providence is finished, life becomes much less painful. Because what's the use
of getting so worked up, you can't change providence, can you. You can't
just grab hold of providence by the throat and say to it, make me happy.
(She throttles an imaginary throat.)

No, and in a way I understand about Kurti and Hannelore. Beautiful memories are so much a part of love. Kurti often said to me, Hannelore's as beautiful now as you were, when you were a girl. Of course it
was wrong, what went on there, and anyway Hannelore was too young
at that stage. But you have to understand Kurti as well. He was such a
handsome officer in the war, he was so proud, and he must have felt, when
we had those victories at the beginning, that the whole world was going
to belong to someone like him. The whole of the rest of his life he never

got rid of that taste he had for victory. And then when Hannelore went off to Australia, he divorced me and married that Chinese or Thailander, whatever she is. I've never understood that, what he could have seen in a slit-eyed eighteen-year-old.

How Miss Brenda Lou Turpin Became Miss Save The Babies And A Star For Jesus

Kristan Ryan

Scene: The sidewalk outside an abortion clinic
Serio-Comic
Miss Save the Babies (forties), a crusader.

> *Here, a foot soldier in the war against abortion explains how she discovered her avocation and her unusual name.*

SAVE THE BABIES: If you had told me when I was a child that every newspaperman in Georgia would want to interview me and that my name would be spoken with reverence from one end of the state to the other, why I'd have thought you were dreaming . . . but I'm proud to say that the Lord has given me the job of *(She scoops the air with her net.)* scooping up the women of the world whose first thought is to rip out their own flesh and blood and save them from drowning in a river of delight and self-gratification. God has made me an instrument of love and salvation and I have become the one and only, Miss Save The Babies.
(She bows her head for a moment as if she is praying and then lifts it and speaks.)

For those of you poor souls who find yourself in a shameful quandary, I want you to know that it's in the safety of the Save the Babies headquarters, just a block south of River Street, where you can learn everything there is to know about the evils of aborting your precious jewel, about abortions gone haywire, see videos of abortions in progress, and be privy to every one of those terrible truths that the pro-choice people don't want you to know. That's right, these folks won't tell you that their doctors pierce little babies' skulls and suck their brains out with rubber hoses, but I will. And why don't they want you to know? Because they can't bear the thought of people like me in the world running around sharing the truth. They want to continue to live in the land of Sodom and Gomorrah, having sex like wild rabbits with anybody they please and doing what they will with the results of their undisciplined hormones.

(Pauses, then goes on cheerfully.)

But I'm getting ahead of myself now. Some of you have asked me to tell you how I came to be the instrument of our Lord and a star for Jesus so I am here today to share with you my blessed story.

Growing up, all I wanted to do was stay in my hometown, have babies, but praise the Lord, I was born without a womb to hold those precious angels. But this is not as bad as it sounds, for yes, indeed, the Lord had something else in mind for me, and because of his great plan here I am, speaking to you today.

(Pause, adjusts her dress and switches her fisherman's net from one hand to the other.)

My birth name *was* Brenda Lou Turpin, until the morning I stepped out of my sister's church onto the sidewalks of Savannah, Georgia and saw that gentleman in his battered old Buick Regal with bloody baby dolls hanging out of a bucket attached to the top and "Thou Shalt Not Kill" scrawled on it's side. I knew that God had answered my prayers about what to do with my life now that my husband of twenty-two years had left me for a waitress from Virgil's Roadside Cafe down in Alabama and I was sent to live with my widowed sister and her four small children on the shores of the Savannah River. When I saw that gentleman wave his hand at me and when he yelled, "Sister, stop the killing," I knew right then why I'd never been able to have children of my own and that finally, God had shined his light on me, that I had been saved for a special purpose. Then I heard the Lord say to me, "Brenda Lou Turpin, thou shall call thyself Miss Save The Babies, and thou will go to the nearest fishing supply store and buy thyself a fisherman's net and a straw fisherman's hat and cover it with the bloodied arms and legs of the baby dolls *(She pats her hat.)* and then take thyself out into the world and put an end to the killing of the innocent growing in the sanctity of the womb."

(Beat.)

Of course, when the Lord tells you to do something, you've got to do it. After all, at any second he could squash any one of us like the bugs we are and I, for one, certainly didn't want to incur the wrath of the Lord and have the life torn from me like a moth flying straight into a bug zapper, so as you can see, I followed his instructions to the letter.

It wasn't a week later when I was down on the riverfront carrying the Lord's message of saving the babies that a reporter from the Atlanta

Constitution stops me on the sidewalk and asks me if I am serious and I say, "When it comes to the Lord, his directives, and the lives of the helpless who are barely formed there is nothing more serious, nothing at all," and then he asks me, "What makes you do this?" And I say, "The Lord makes me, he shows me the way. He told me to tell the world to stop the aspiration of fetuses and he places his words on my tongue so that the world will hear him speak. Why, sir, I have a vision of leading the way to salvation for those young girls and women who are lost to the sorrow of pierced navels and tongues, midriff tops, thong panties, and the feel of flesh against flesh and I mean to stop it all and save the babies begotten of lust and sport sex." And he says, "What's your name?" "Why it's Miss Save The Babies," I told him proud as punch, and it was then that I heard the Lord say, "See an attorney and change thy name *legally* to "Save The Babies."

(Pause.)

So he asks me, "Is that your legal name?" And I say, "It's not yet, but the Lord told me to change it legally and just as soon as the Lord gives me enough money I'll go to court and get my name change taken care of."

(Pause.)

So this man who is my age and who I do not know counts out five twenty dollar bills and hands them to me and says, "Is that enough?" And I say, "Why hallelujah, yes, sir, I think it might be," and while I am peering into his eyes to see if I can spot a little bit of heaven, Mr. Reporter says to me, "How'd you like to come to my hotel room and let me interview you? I'll give you another hundred bucks, if you'll spend an hour talking to me." Then he tells me that he was once party to a young girl's downfall and maybe he can earn a place in the Lord's house by writing an article about me. Naturally, I know then that the Lord is speaking through this handsome stranger with curly gray-blond hair and cool blue eyes and that this man in his three-piece designer suit is a tool of Jesus himself, so I go straight to my sister's house, brush my teeth and put on a clean black dress, say "see ya later" to her children who are screaming their heads off for something to eat, and head to the hotel to do the Lord's work and save the babies by getting my message out to more people in one day than I see in a week at this clinic right here.

(Waving her hand behind her indicating the clinic and then looking to heaven.)

Now, I am a savior myself, a fisher of you women and young girls who are about to send yourselves straight to Hades for tearing your unwanted children from your loins and throwing them in the trash like spoiled meat. I carry this net *(She points to her net.)* as a symbol of our saviour the Lord Jesus Christ who reaches out to each and every one of you lost souls, who scoops you into his arms to deliver you from the evils of Satan and from the fires of hell by committing the crime of murder. I am the tool of the Lord and the purpose of my life has never been so clear. Amen.

Hunger

Sheri Wilner

Scene: A beach house

Dramatic

Diana (twenties to thirties), a young woman on the verge of metamorphosis.

Diana and her fiancé have arrived at the beach house for a romantic get-away and to celebrate their engagement. When he asks her what she was staring at in the waves on the ferry ride to the island, she offers the following answer.

DIANA: I was watching the foam.

[ADAM: Foam? Interesting. For two hours?]

DIANA: I could see my shadow. First in the water, but then I noticed it was really vivid, really easy to see in the foam. And I started imagining that it wasn't my reflection I was seeing. I started imagining that it was the silhouette of my body I could see from above. Did you ever see when they film dolphins from above like that? You just see this shadowy gray form racing through the water. That's what I started seeing. Except it was me, not a dolphin. And it felt like I was swimming. Fast. As fast as dolphins swim. But because I was sitting down, the shape of my silhouette didn't make sense. I was definitely sitting in a chair, not swimming. So I had this incredible urge to spread out like this. *(She demonstrates — stretching her arms and legs straight out.)* Like Superman so the image on the water matched the image in my mind.

Hunger
Sheri Wilner

Scene: A beach house
Dramatic
Diana (twenties to thirties), a young woman on the verge of metamorphosis.

> *Diana is suffering from a crisis of faith in her own existence. When their romantic getaway begins to go awry, she makes the following startling confession to her fiancé.*

DIANA: I don't belong with anyone.

[ADAM: What does that mean? Huh? Diana, what does that mean?]

DIANA: I don't belong anywhere. Everywhere I go I feel like a trespasser. Like at any moment sirens will start blaring at me and guard dogs will start barking.

[ADAM: Why?]

DIANA: And every time I move, I feel such a . . . resistance. I have such trouble moving through the air. I push myself through and it always feels like I'm scraping against sharp edges that no one else ever seems to feel. And sometimes I feel so clogged up inside that I can't breathe and there is so much force pushing against my lungs that I'm afraid they'll collapse. No, I want them to collapse. And I stand here and I look at the ocean and all I can think about is how much more I'd prefer to be there than here.

Hunger
Sheri Wilner

Scene: A beach house
Dramatic
Diana (twenties to thirties), a young woman on the verge of metamorphosis.

Here, Diana reveals that she longs to enter the ocean and never return.

DIANA: I look at the ocean and . . . and all I want to do is be far, far out in the middle of the water. Nothing for miles and miles but water. And while I'm floating, I want to feel the pores of my skin start to open, wide . . . wide . . . wide. And I want them to grow until they're the size of mouths and they open and close and open and close and water flows in them and through the inside of my body and then back out. I am completely porous, completely open. And I don't need to push, or kick, or swim. I don't need muscles. The water carries me, it passes me from arm to arm all the while stroking my hair, all the while filling me up with warmth and calmness. *(The sound of Diana's longing can now be heard under her speech.)*
And slowly I begin to dissolve and spread out far throughout the sea further and further, so in between each miniscule part of me is miles and miles and miles and I keep dissolving and spreading out, dissolving and spreading out, until each part of me is smaller than a molecule of water and then I fall inside the molecules and they carry me. Translucent balloons that I float inside and carry me throughout the sea. And I float and float and float and float.

Just a Little Fever
Caitlin Hicks

Scene: Here and now
Dramatic
Dorothy (thirties to forties), a woman whose marriage is in jeopardy.

Here, Dorothy laments the changes perpetrated on her body by pregnancy and her husband's subsequent disinterest in intimacy.

DOROTHY: Yesterday, when the twins were having a nap, it hit me like a lead brick. I was sitting in the tub looking at that cameo photograph of Sam and me on our wedding day, and I suddenly realized how completely our relationship had changed!

It occurred to me that it happened almost overnight when the twins were born. Things were never quite the same after the twins were born. I was entirely consumed by their presences; I couldn't look at him and feel anything for him in the first week of their lives! It alarmed me at the time, but I was so busy with the twins, the days slipped right by.

Then, yesterday, surrounded by all that warm water, I looked at that white dress and the shape of my body, and for the first time wondered what Sam thinks when he sees me naked in our bedroom. How could that hopeful little girl have been me?

I stood up in the tub and saw my slippery reflection in those marbleized mirrors. What a sense of loss I felt! There are things about my body that are changed forever because of the twins. My legs, for instance, they're a mess! Especially around the ankles. The veins are quite soft. I don't think he can feel them in the dark, but they're hard to miss in the daylight. I remember looking at them and thinking they were stuck to someone else's legs. But in fact, they're stuck to my legs!

Sitting there, alone in the soapy water next to our wedding picture. Remembering one night when the twins were about three months old: Pammy was gulping air in the next room, my ears were ringing, and I don't know, it looked like we could both use a bit of comfort. I was lying on my stomach with Sam's pillow over my head, and the smell of Sam's pillow! Suddenly it came back to me! How it was the first time we made love! I turned over and touched him on the inside of his leg, like he likes. I must have been feeling pretty low, because just doing a little thing like that made me cry. But he just rolled over, like there was no one there.

Sitting there in the bathtub, remembering how the bare trees bent a shadow across his shoulders, I realized: I have been alone in our bed for quite some time now.

Just a Little Fever

Caitlin Hicks

Scene: Here and now

Dramatic

Dorothy (thirties to forties), a woman whose marriage is in jeopardy.

Here, Dorothy recalls a photograph that perfectly captured the love that she and her husband once shared.

DOROTHY: So it seems odd to me that as he strokes my hair, I should remember a bright and turquoise photograph of the two of us, tanned by a sparkling pool, and the specific taste of a grape drink we shared in Phoenix that summer we met. I can taste it! I can feel the hot, dry air baking onto my skin. I can taste the purple sweetness as it spills onto my lips and is brushed away by his. His lips were so soft! He was just a junior high school teacher! He wasn't a big trader! He wasn't pursued by politicians and women for his money! He was just a man, and he looked into my eyes when we made love with each other!

In this half-light, I am looking at his broad face. His lips are curling at the edges into a gentle smile as he waits for my body to shift over him. He receives me. I receive him. My back is pressed against his belly, his arms surround mine. The sound of his windly breath is full and building in my ears. It seems odd to be kissing his hands, his arms, with a loving rhythm, but I am kissing this particular man, my husband, like I want him to know me. And I can sense that he is with me in our bed at this moment.

It seems odd that under his fervent touch, my breasts are hot and my thighs are wet. But now I understand something! This moment is all I have! In this present moment, I am living my life. And under this measured, defeated slowness we share in the shadow of our loss, it seems like there is some love left between us.

And if there is, I would like to embrace it.

Just a Little Fever
Caitlin Hicks

Scene: Here and now
Dramatic
Karen (thirties), a woman haunted by a frightening memory.

Here, Karen recalls a tragic day from her childhood that continues to affect her view of reality.

KAREN: That's me, the one with the crown on my head. My Daddy used to call me his little princess. I guess I look like a princess in that picture. I was ten. That's my mother at the piano. She would play for me in the afternoons after school. Once a week, I went to ballet lessons and the rest of the week, except Saturday and Sunday, I would move the furniture, push back the rug and just dance! My mother sat at the bench, humming, and I would get on my pink tights and my slippers and just leap and jump and twirl across the floor! She pretended only to be looking at the music, but now I'm sure she watched me from the corner of her eye. In winter, on Sundays, we went skating together. In summer, we went on holidays, usually driving somewhere.

On one of those trips, when I was eleven, we were travelling through Texas, and we stopped at a steakhouse by the road. It was this tacky place with stuffed bears and antlered deer and buffalo hanging on the wall, and they had this running bet with anyone who came in the door! If you could eat thirty-two ounces of steak in less than an hour, your meal was free! But we were too hot for that! I was picking at my meat, and they started arguing, so I plugged up my ears with my fingers. Then, my Mother, who was sitting next to me, pushed herself from the table. Something was wrong, because suddenly she was quiet. I looked up: she had her hands around her neck, and she was trying to talk! To breathe! She looked so surprised! She was panicking at Daddy, fear in her eyes, and hope too. My Dad just stood there, his arms outstretched. I ran to him, he pushed me away, and from the floor I could see her feet stumbling around on the dirty carpet until she fell. All the shoes and legs gathering around, shuffling, hypnotized in a circle. I crawled to her leg, kissing it, kissing it, kissing it! Trying to save her! I was just a kid, there was nothing I could do! I kept seeing that look on her face: "Please! Do something! Save me!" it said. And my Dad! So lamely reaching across the table, like a beggar. The men can't save us!

Just a Little Fever
Caitlin Hicks

Scene: Here and now
Dramatic
Karen (thirties), a woman haunted by a frightening memory.

After a frustrating attempt to quiet someone else's baby, pregnant Karen here confesses fear about the arrival of her own.

KAREN: It's humorous, if you think about it. A grown person, an intelligent, skilled, functioning BEING at the mercy of a squalling baby! Jesus! I didn't know she would spook when she saw me! What was I going to do? I did the obvious, give her a bottle, thank god there was one already milked up in the refrigerator. She spit it out. Right, it was freezing! So I warmed it under the faucet and meanwhile, she is screaming, screaming, screaming! Incessantly, this shrill, unnerving, high decibel repetitive SOUND. It woke up the baby in my gut. Suddenly I'm feeling this thing pushing an elbow under my rib. Some people are just not cut out for it. I'm one of them.

Where is Sam tonite? Who is he thinking about?

Once again, something is happening to me. I hate that! When I don't happen to it, it happens to me. It's frightening. There is a certain thrill to it, but it brings me right back to the dirty carpet and my mother's feet like nothing else.

To be attached to someone, without choice, to feel deep and strong feelings: love? Panic! To be standing helpless outside of that person, compelled to watch while it happens! Right in front of your face! To be unable to escape! The vulnerability is unbearable.

The Memory of Water

Shelag Stephenson

Scene: Here and now
Dramatic
Teresa (thirty to forty), a woman grieving for her mother.

Here, traumatized Teresa describes her horrifying experience in the hospital the night her mother died.

TERESA: I think I'm going mad.

[CATHERINE: Last night I dreamed I could do yogic flying. I bet that means something — *(She tugs at the jacket.)* I'm not sure about this, are you? I don't suit black, that's the problem.]

TERESA: As soon as the phone went I knew.

[CATHERINE: Can you wear trousers at a funeral?]

TERESA: I said to Frank, I can't answer it. We should never have left her at the hospital like that. We should have stayed.

[MARY: You weren't to know.]

TERESA: I'm not good with hospitals, I had to get away. Everyone in her ward looked like they'd already died, everyone was pale grey with a catheter. *(Mary is opening the mail. Reads.)*

[MARY: "With deepest sympathy on your sad loss, Mimi." Who's Mimi?]

TERESA: When Frank spoke to them they said, she's worse, you'd better get up to the hospital. I took the phone and said, she's dead isn't she, you don't phone at three in the morning unless someone's dead. And this, this is the awful bit, I put the phone down, and the next thing I wanted to do more than anything else was have sex, which is sick, I know, that's what Frank said afterwards. I know I should have phoned you two, but I had this idea, this flicker she might not be dead, even though I knew she was really, but they wouldn't tell me over the phone, and I'd have woken you up, and what would the point be anyway, you were miles away —

[MARY: It's OK. Stop worrying about it —]

TERESA: That's why I didn't phone straight away. Mimi used to live three doors down.

[CATHERINE: Can I borrow a skirt from someone?]

TERESA: I keep going over and over it —

[CATHERINE: Is anyone listening to me?]

[MARY: Oh, shut up and sit down. Your cyst might burst.]

TERESA: And the doctor was about twelve, and embarrassed. Eventually we had to say it for him. He kept fiddling with his pen and giving us a rundown of everything that had happened, until eventually Frank said, "Are you trying to tell us she's not coming back? Are you trying to tell us she's dead?" And he said, "More or less, yes." And I said, what d'you mean, more or less? She's either dead or she isn't, you can't be a bit dead, for God's sake." And then I looked at my feet and I was wearing odd shoes. A black one and a brown one. Not even vaguely similar. So I started to laugh and I couldn't stop. They had to give me a sedative. Frank was shocked. They're not like us, his family, they've got Italian blood. Someone dies, they cry. They don't get confused and laugh.

The Memory of Water
Shelag Stephenson

Scene: Here and now
Serio-Comic
Catherine (twenties to thirties), a woman who has just been dumped by her
  boyfriend.

*Catherine has a problem maintaining a relationship with a man as she here
confesses to her sisters.*

CATHERINE: Fuck it! *(Silence. She bursts into racking sobs.)* I went to this coun-
  selor — did I tell you this? — or a therapist or something and she said
  I had this problem and the problem was, I give too much, I just do too
  much for other people, I'm just a very giving person, and I never get any
  credit for any of it. I haven't even got any friends. I mean, I have but I
  don't like most of them, especially the women, and I try really hard, it's
  just I'm very sensitive and I get taken for a ride, nothing, ever goes right,
  every time, I mean, every time it's the same — like with men. What is it
  with men? I mean, I don't have a problem with men or anything. I love
  men. I've been to bed with seventy-eight of them, I counted, so obvi-
  ously there's not a problem or anything, it's just he didn't even apologize
  or anything and how can he say on the phone he doesn't want to see me
  anymore? I mean, why now? Why couldn't he have waited? I don't know
  what to do, why does it always go wrong? I don't want to be on my own,
  I'm sick of people saying I'm better off on my own, I'm not that sort of
  person, I can't do it. I did everything for him, I was patient and all the
  things you're supposed to be and people kept saying don't accept this from
  him, don't accept that, like, you know, when he stayed out all night, not
  very often, I mean once or twice, and everyone said tell him to fuck off,
  but how could I because what if he did? Because they all do, everyone
  I've ever met does, they all disappear and I don't know if it's me or what.
  I don't want to be on my own, I can't stand it, I know it's supposed to
  be great but I don't think it is. I can't help it, it's no good pretending, it's
  fucking lonely and I can't bear it.

Mrs. Mygoodness

David Fleisher

Scene: A classroom

Serio-Comic

Mrs. Mygoodness (thirty to fifty), a woman who has murdered her husband and two other individuals.

Mrs. Mygoodness is participating in a community service prison release program by teaching a class in Domestic Stability and Gun Control. Here, the convicted killer greets her new class.

MRS. MYGOODNESS: Class. Students. Please settle down. Class?

(Slams pointer against blackboard.)

Class! Thank you. Let's first check and make sure you're in the right place. This is "Domestic Stability and Gun Control." Please check your schedule and make sure this is where you should be. Well, since I see no hands, I assume you're all in the right place. Good. My name is Mrs. Mygoodness. I'm sure you'll all have questions, so please feel free to interrupt at any time. You may have read about me in the newspaper or heard various rumors on campus. I am teaching this course as part of a community service prison release program. At the present time, I'm housed in maximum security for shooting my husband and two other individuals. Class, please settle down.

(Slams pointer against blackboard.)

Class! There's no reason to be alarmed.

(Pointing to audience.)

Yes? A 9-millimeter.

(Pointing.)

Yes, dear? Because the 9-millimeter is quicker and more efficient. Now, let's first look at exactly how domestic stability relates to gun control. Break it down. First, domestic stability. What immediately comes to mind when we think of domestic stability? Compatibility, right? However, you and your loved one may not turn out to be right for each other. Unfortunate, yes, but it happens. In fact, fifty percent of all marriages in this country end in divorce. That's right, class, *fifty* percent. Astounding, isn't it? Now if fifty percent of all marriages end in divorce, what percentage of couples remain married? Feel free to use your calculators.

(Pointing.)

Yes, in the back? Correct. Now given that you have a fifty-fifty chance of getting divorced, doesn't it make sense to be prepared *before* your marriage ends? Which brings us to gun control.

(Pointing.)

Yes? In the bedroom, around midnight. One shot to the head, one in the . . . abdomen. He was pronounced dead at the hospital.

Now, let's look at the relationship between marriage and gun control. Take a hypothetical situation. You and your loved one have a disagreement . . . something trivial . . . say your child is kidnapped. Tempers flare. Harsh words are exchanged. Mean-spirited accusations are made. The television is too loud. The toilet's backed up. You didn't get enough sleep the night before. You've been downsized at work. You need root canal. And the little wife has to throw up again because she just found out she has another unwanted pregnancy. And you aren't the father. All this needs closure.

(Takes a gun out of a duffel bag.)

This is a *small* caliber weapon. Class, please make a note of this, never overreact to a domestic squabble. It can only cause needless bloodshed. You don't have to use a high-powered automatic weapon for a problem as shallow and insignificant as a missing child. A semi-automatic will do just fine.

(Pointing.)

Yes, Hon? Good question. Why not settle the disagreement with a knife? Time consuming, not to mention stabbing requires more energy.

(Pointing.)

Yes? Mr. Simpson was dealing with a more emotionally volatile situation than kidnapping. A knife was the correct weapon of choice in that case because Mr. Simpson was overcome with what emotion, class? Absolutely. Jealousy. The Simpson case also involves male domination. When we combine jealousy with male domination, a large sharp instrument is the correct weapon to employ. It's more intimate. When used properly, it makes a more personal statement.

There's yet another important factor to consider with respect to weapon selection. Would anyone like to venture a guess as to . . .

(Pointing.)

Yes, dear? Finances, of course. Why spend extra money on a more sophisticated weapon when the situation doesn't warrant it? Look, if I could have used a twenty-two on my husband, believe me, I would have.

(Pointing.)

Yes? I caught him in bed with two women. For a split second, I considered a small caliber weapon because one of the women was my sister. My sister and I are very close. But the other woman was his ex-wife. Therefore, I was forced out of necessity to choose a much more powerful firearm. Okay, I've given you a lot to think about. Let's take a break. Breathe in deeply and let the air out, slowly. Go ahead.

(Scans audience.)

That's it. Again.

(She breathes in deeply.)

Life. It's a wonderful thing, isn't it? Now, class, what I want you to do is close your eyes and hold your breath for five seconds. Go ahead, take in a deep breath and hold it. Close your eyes.

(She breaths in deeply, holding it for five seconds.)

Death. So, what we have here is life . . . and death. The next time your loved one says something you don't like, *think* first. Should it be a .22, a .38, a 44-magnum, a 9-millimeter? Think, class, think. It's a matter of sizing up the situation and making the appropriate weapon selection based on the content and seriousness of the dispute. Finally, never underestimate the value of a good defense lawyer.

Now, your assignment for next week. Before we know how to employ responsible gun control in the home, we must, first, do what, class? Practice. I want you to approach someone you don't know, a complete stranger, and engage that individual in an argument. The dispute, itself, can be about anything, doesn't matter, but preferably something that provokes intense anger. Once emotions escalate to an intolerable level, shoot the individual. Then write a five-hundred-word essay, describing the incident in detail.

We'll read aloud your essay and offer constructive criticism. Look, I know the temptation to cheat. So, to prove you have really done the assignment, sever a body part from the slain individual and attach it to your essay. It can be a foot, arm, nose, eyeball . . . whatever. Questions? Fine. See you next week.

Nude Monologue

Jeff Goode

Scene: A theater
Serio-Comic
Actress/dancer (twenty to thirty).

> *Here, an actress explains how she came to be performing in the nude.*

> *Enter dancer.*
> *Removes all clothing.*
> *Looks at audience.*

ACTRESS/DANCER: Am I boring you?
  (Takes a pose.)

I'm sorry, It can't be helped.

I had planned, you know, to entertain you.

I had costumes and jewelry.
And a box of chickens.

They took away my chickens.
Too suggestive.

I offered to encase them in latex. But they wouldn't hear it.

"No chickens," they said.
"Chickens are not to be trusted."

Especially
. . . the cocks.
You never know what they'll doodle do.

"A chicken is not wholesome."

Unless it's fried.
And they whisked them away.

To be fried, presumably.

So you won't see any chickens tonight.

"Now about the clothes," they said.

"These clothes?" I asked,
gesturing toward my wardrobe of red and black leather gear.

"Yes, *those*," they said.
As if they were afraid to touch them even with their words.
"These?" I said. "Those," they said.
"These?" "Those."
"These right here?" "Those, yes, those!" *(With disgust.)* "Those . . . *clothes*."

What about 'em?

Well, they said. You can't wear them.
Of course I can, I said, and I offered to demonstrate how to fit five inches
of spandex around a thirty-five inch waist.
No, no, no, they clarified.
It's not that you *can't* wear them. You seem quite limber.
But you can't be *allowed* to wear them.
It can't be permitted. Condoned.
It's unethical. Unacceptable.
Unseemly.

Really? I asked. Unethical? I asked.

Because of the crucifix embroidered across the codpiece?

Oh, no, it's not that, they stammered. We hadn't even noticed that. No,
it's just that it's . . . too revealing.

But how can that be? I asked.
All my nasty bits are covered.
My nipples.
My . . . well, you know — the nasty bits.

Yes, we see that, they said. You've covered all your bases quite nicely.

I was flattered.

But it's not the bases that worry us. It's the basepaths.

Yes, those unbroken expanses of flesh leave nothing to the imagination.

Well, I wouldn't call it nothing, but I didn't want to argue, so I offered
to substitute a fishnet body stocking which breaks up the flesh into nice
bite-sized chunks. Or a skintight outfit I would make with spray paint
and a handful of sequins.
But they wouldn't have any of it.

The simple fact is. You can't wear any of these costumes.

That's all right, I said.
Art is art.
I'll do the show in jeans and a t-shirt.

That's what we like to hear. Jeans and a t-shirt. But, oh, you don't mean
that t-shirt you're wearing?

Well, it doesn't have to be this one. Why? Is there a hole in the fabric? Is
my chest hair protruding in an undignified manner. Is my turtleneck col-
lar slung too low in back?
What —
they quavered with great timidity —
is that thing emblazoned across your chest?

Oh, this? Oh, it's nothing. A slogan. A saying. Just something I believe
in.

Beliefs? Oh no! they shrieked.

You mustn't believe.

Or at least, they looked around to be sure the Constitution hadn't over-heard them. You mustn't let anyone know you believe. It is, after all, a free country.

Thank God! I said.

Yes, but not in public.

Smoking, religion, sex. These are things which must be confined to the privacy of one's own bedroom. They said. If then . . . Especially the smok-ing.

I see, and I take it the same goes for political statements.

Well, at this point, someone fainted and had to be carried out on a stretcher, so I decided not to press the subject.

I offered to wear a t-shirt blank on both sides so as not to make any po-litical statements at all, but they peered at me warily and told me that that smacked of protest.

And the only thing worse than dissension is outright subversion.

As they chuckled at the absurdity of my naive suggestion, I laughed along with them.

Well, I said, if I'm going to do this show, I have to wear something. Can you suggest anything that might be appropriate?

Nothing at all, they said.

And with that, they filed out without even discussing my text.

The One
Jolene Goldenthal

Scene: Here and now
Dramatic
Woman (thirty to fifty), a frustrated political coach.

Here, a woman watches the candidate she's coached while knowing that she could do much better herself.

WOMAN: Take it slow I tell her. Smile a lot. Like this. I show her. *(She smiles sweetly, slowly.)* One sentence at a time. Then smile. Slowly. *(She smiles again, demonstrating.)*

Wait for them to clap. *(Pause.)* Sure they will. Of course they will. You're up there. You're waiting. You're smiling at them. They know what they're supposed to do. Put their hands together and . . . *Right!*

Now again. Nice and slow. That's good. That's good. That's very good. Now remember — that's no brain trust out there. It's people. Just people. Give them a chance. They want to like you. They *need* to like you. They're looking for a hero and you may be it. You may be THE ONE, I tell her. You may be IT. *(Pause.)*

I tell her. And I tell her. And I tell her again. She's getting it. She's getting better. But oh my God so s-l-o-w-l-y.

I could do it upside down. Standing on my head. Blindfolded. Shackled. *(Gesture.)* But *she's* the one. Not me. Oh, yeah. Nearly forgot the clothes. Keep it simple I tell her. Look good but not too good. Someplace between Vogue and The Inquirer. And the hair. Simple. Neat. That's it. Forget glamour. Forget everything. Watch the TelePrompter. But smile while you're doing it. *(Pause.)* Hey, listen. I'm not the speechwriter. I'm only the coach. She's the one.

I'm the last link before the big test. I prep her for the public. I urge her on. I push-pull her through it. "Come on!" I say over and over. "You can do it. Yes you can! Yes you can!"

And she can. She will. Eventually. I hope. Hey, this is my job here. I get paid to do this. But oh migod . . . I watch her and I suffer. I watch her work through it over and over . . . So carefully. So painfully. And I see myself out there. Not her. Me.

Head up. Shoulders back. Smile, baby, smile. *I would be terrific!* And you'd love me. All of you. I'd make you love me. *(Pause.)* But I'm not the one. I'm not running for anything. I'm not looking for your vote, ladies and gentlemen. I'm only the coach. She's the one.

BUT I WOULD BE SO GOOD! I'm a *natural!* Why can't they see that? Why don't they know that? Maybe they can't hear me. Maybe I need to tell them . . . Look. Forget her. CHOOSE ME! CHOOSE ME! *I'M THE ONE!*

Past Tense Feminine Gender
Le Wilhelm

Scene: Various New Year's Eves
Serio-Comic
Alma (fifteen to twenty), a young woman welcoming in the twentieth century.

On New Year's Eve 1899, Alma has stolen away from her parent's party to quietly reflect on what the future may bring.

ALMA: It's a beautiful night. Not a cloud in the sky. Looking out the window you see a zillion stars. I don't know if I have ever seen a finer night than this. There's snow on the ground and the light from the moon and stars reflects off the white land.

I'm all dressed up because it's New Year's Eve. This dress was made by a company in Philadelphia. It's my first dress that I've ever had that wasn't made by my momma. I like it a lot, but I like a dress that's made by my momma too, 'cause I get to watch it being born. And I get to try it on and even make suggestions sometimes when she's in a good mood.

In just a few seconds it will be a brand new century!! You can probably hear them downstairs. That's where the party's going on. I snuck up here to the attic room so I could be by myself. I love it up here. I always go here when I want to be alone. I also like to look out the window at the hills and the river. Tonight I'm up here waiting for the 20th century to arrive.

Because it's a new century, everyone has been acting strange, real excited and planning big parties. Well, that's what most people are doing. Some folks in town have said that this is the end of time. That Jesus is going to come back and take the good people with him and the bad people are going to get judged and then they're going to get burned. Burned for all eternity, that's what they say. My parents don't believe that's going to happen and neither do I, so they're having a party.

I feel kind of sorry for all those people who believe the world's going to end 'cause when it don't, I guess they're going to be terribly disappointed and feel downright foolish. I know I would!! If I had gone around telling everyone the end is near, and then the end doesn't end. I'd feel like an idiot.

You probably think it's odd that I don't want to be downstairs at the party with my friends and family where all the fun's going on. And I can't stay up here long, because someone's going to miss me and come looking for me, worrying about me, thinking that I must be sad or scared. But I don't know. I just want to be by myself. So I can remember it. I want to be able to remember when the twentieth century dawned.

I know it's just a date on a calendar. I know that . . . but still it's a new century . . . my century — it's when I'm going to live most of my life . . . and no one knows what's going to happen . . . there'll be hundreds of thousands of things . . . all kinds of changes . . . all sorts of wonderful things . . . things that I'm going to be a part of. I'm curious and I'm scared . . . and I'm excited . . .

(Cast begins counting, as does she.) Nine, eight, seven, six, five, four, three, two — one — Happy New Year!

Past Tense Feminine Gender

Le Wilhelm

Scene: Various New Year's Eves

Serio-Comic

Leigh (thirty to forty), a woman greeting the twenty-first century.

Leigh has mixed feelings about the new millennium as she here reveals.

LEIGH: *(She toasts.)* Happy fucking New Year. God, I can't tell you now good it felt to say that. I've been pushed onto the bridge that leads to the 21st century and now I've been drug across it.

The problem is that some time in February of 1999, all the hype for the new millennium did me in. I'm not quite sure where it happened, but I know there was a time when I was watching the television and those damn millennium M&M candies were jabbering on and I tuned out.

Of course the phone's rung off the hook today. People calling asking what I'm going to do. Am I going out? Asking if I'm watching the celebration on the television — did I see such and such with Peter Jennings — Tom Brokaw — Dan Rather — Cokie Roberts — Ted Koppel — Did I hear such and such millionaire-billionaire singer — wasn't it wonderful? And I tried to do those things. I watched the first dawn of the twenty-first century as the clock struck twelve in some remote part of Oceania . . . and I felt nothing . . . but I stuck with it, and the phone started ringing even more somewhere around New Zealand-Australia and it got to be just a little more than I could take . . . I turned off Peter-Dan-Cokie-Tom-Ted, took the phone off the hook and went to bed for the rest of the afternoon.

As you may have noted, I'm not in the best of moods — I often get a little testy around the New Year — I'm single — and I'm never quite sure how I'm supposed to act — I don't know about anyone else, but I think New Year's dates are the worst. I have a lot of friends who like to copulate themselves into the next year — it's their New Year's tradition —I tried it a couple of times, but it all seemed too forced, too planned.

But this year's mood is worse than usual. Everything's changing so fast now, with all the new technology — it truly is a whole new world that is constantly changing, expanding, then shrinking. It's as if we're once more in the age of the Pioneers when no one is sure what will happen next.

All of that truly is what the problem with today comes down to. I'm not old. But in terms of decades I don't have that many left, three or four. That's about all, unless there's some miracle in medicine — and I can't trust in that — and when I think about this, it makes me angry and bitter because I won't be there for all the wonderful things that'll happen in those decades after I'm gone. And I want to be there. I want to experience it all.

When I stop and think of all the changes that took place during the 20th century, especially for women, it is truly overwhelming. I always try to live here and now and not dwell on what's already happened — but tonight is different — it's the dawning of the twenty-first century and now maybe that we've said Happy New Year, it's time for a little retrospection — a little trek into the past tense, feminine gender of the twentieth century.

Past Tense Feminine Gender

Le Wilhelm

Scene: Various New Year's Eves
Serio-Comic
Kelsey (fourteen), a young girl suffering from depressive ennui.

Kelsey has managed to pack a lot of living into her fourteen years leaving her feeling a bit like Peggy Lee when she asked the question: "Is That All There Is?" Here, Kelsey reveals her plans of self-destruction.

KELSEY: I'm fourteen. Had a birthday last month. Went to New Orleans with some people. Live down the street. The colonial two story. One with the chain link. One with the Porsche in the driveway.

The Porsche is mom's. Dad drives a BMW. She's an attorney. Corporate law. Sounds like a drag to me. She must like it, she's there till all hours. Dad's into manufacturing. Most of his companies are overseas. He's out of town a lot. He took me with him once. It wasn't a big deal. We went to China. Shanghai. I was bored.

I got into trouble a couple years back. I'm not sure mom and dad remember it. Expelled. For smoking pot with David Cohen. I was lucky they didn't find the crack. I don't get the crack rage. Crack's no big deal to me. I smoked it. I can take it or leave it. I don't see why people find it addictive. Tell you the truth, it was a big disappointment to me. Lots of things are that way.

Most everything that everyone thinks is so rad — I find drab. Sex is like that. Sex, what's the big deal? Girls sitting around saying they'll score this one or that one. My friend Ashley has a honest-to-goodness scorecard, lots of my friends have them. The idea is to fill the scorecard. They tried to get me to do it. I blew them off. I got better things to do than fuck a bunch of douchebags. Lot better things to do, like clip my toenails.

I just love the fucking talking heads on TV who always are saying what's wrong with the children of today . . . bunch of talking heads . . . who were probably the ones who never got into trouble . . . they want to understand kids today . . . then you'd think they'd go to the source . . . it's all just such a fucking drag . . . that's how we all feel . . . America was founded by a bunch of racist bigots, white people are the scum of the earth and God is dead, and anyone who believes in Christianity is weak-minded. Repeat after me, Christianity is for the weak-minded, America is founded by a bunch of racists, we are all scum, God is dead and I don't feel so good. They ought to be able to turn that into a rap song, don't you think?

'Course it's all really a bore. Like when someone thinks they're doing something rad by getting some part of their body pierced. I had my belly button pierced, but I don't wear the stud any more. Everyone I know has a piercing of some kind or another. Lots of girls have them on their privates. I don't. I think that's trying just a little too much. What's the point?

Sometimes I cut myself . . . not deep but just cut myself. You know, for the hell of it. I have scars on my arms and on my legs. No one ever notices. Actually the school nurse noticed, but I made up some story. 'Course she didn't believe it, but she acted like she did so she wouldn't have to bother. And that's the best. No one gives a fuck . . . especially me.

I don't plan on hanging around too long. I don't see what all of this is about. Life, I'm talking about now. If I live past twenty, I'll really be a jag off. Anyone who doesn't kill themselves or die before twenty, they're a real loser. Why the hell would anyone want to hang around this place?

Pompei

Bob Jude Ferrante

Scene: Here and now
Serio-Comic
Cassandra (twenty to forty), a traveler.

Here, a visionary woman recalls an encounter in Pompei.

CASSANDRA: Some time
    (If you do turn out to have some time)
    Take a side-trip
    to see Pompei.
    Cute little town.
    A little *too* little.

    The bus arrives.
    It's always an ash-grey day
    there in Pompei.
    And Vesuvio,
    sports a worn pair of tan corduroys
    smokes pack after pack of Parliaments
    placid, barely notices you,
    just kisses the ball
    and hurls it against the sand.
    Baci!

    You walk around Pompei for hours.
    Trying to find a decent cheeseburger
    Good luck there, kiddo.

    You bump into this guy, a local.
    He's really . . . stoned.
    Try to talk to him.
    He doesn't answer.
    He crouches.

And covers his face.
Like this.
(Takes the position of a petrified Pompeian.)

Must be embarrassed
(stoned so early in the day.
Isn't everyone?)

You ask the guy, "Tell me. What happened?"

Finally he speaks.
He says, "Happened?"
And shoots you with that
"you Americas think you know everything, don't you?" look.
He says, "A flood, that's what *happened.*"

And you ask, "A flood? Of water? It's dry. Of what?"

He says, "Not really. Of words."

So you think,
now here's something.
A flood. Of words.
And you ask, "What were they like?
Good words?
Profound? Philosophical?
Descriptive? Literate?"

And he thinks a moment, then says,
"Not really,
They started small, here and there.
Articles mostly.
A. The. An.
So at first nobody noticed.
But as the words gathered
they got longer
like chains of nucleotides.

Particles. Gerunds.
Conjugated verbs.
Obfuscation.
Fastidiousness.
Quotidian diatribes.
Soon there were rivulets: Sentences.
Then streams: Paragraphs.
The tide rose. It picked things up: Pages floated past.
Volumes.
Shelves.
A few people saw them, but everyone said, 'words? Get a job.'
Then a few more people saw them and there started to be rumors.
Which were just more words."

"The tide got deeper.
But it was Monday. They had to do their job.
So they went to their job."

"They came home at six,
looking forward to dinner and TV."

"By then the words were a lake deep and wide,
so you could hardly see across.
Whole library shelves filled with flood."

"But hey, the folks were tired.
It was a long hard day at the job.
They went to bed,
listening to the comforting sounds of the waves
against the shores of their dreaming minds."

"Some maybe wanted to buy furniture and cars,
but ended up buying boats
But I guess they all sank."

And that was all there was to his story.
Which was more words.

He resumes crouching
And you resume your quest for a snack.

When you get back home,
where there's a snack on practically every corner,
you remember your visits to Pompei.
And think,
"Maybe some day Pompei will come visit me at home?"
It would be more convenient.
You could watch the banks as they rise.
And listen to the sounds of waves pounding the beach.
And ask, "What time is it?"

And the Pompeians will answer,
their words bubbling to the surface of their private sea
"It's time to wake up, time to get a job.
Time to watch. Watch. Watch."
(Slide: a watch second hand moving around.)
"Watch."
(SFX: Sound of ticking.)

Pretty

Alison Diana Meehan

Scene: Here and now

Dramatic

Elizabeth (twenties), a young woman struggling to balance love and self-image.

Here, Elizabeth describes her destructive relationship with her mother and the surprise of love.

ELIZABETH: I asked my mother one day if I was pretty. It is a question that all little girls ask their mothers at one point. Only mother said that I wasn't. My mother told me that I would never be pretty, and that god and the people who saw me knew that I was a bad little girl and that was why I was cursed with being ugly. I cried when I heard that and I tried to be good. I hoped that god would make me pretty like my mother and my sister. Then my mother died. The last time I saw her she told me that I had better do well in school because there was no way I would ever find a husband, then she told my sister to wait for a doctor or a lawyer or someone with a trust fund. I was 12 when she died. I missed my mother more than anyone else. The moment after she died my sister kept on reminding me that I would never be pretty. I started to hate my sister. It came to the point where because of her I stopped caring how I looked or how I did in school, I tried to make my family ashamed of me. I lived like I had no home until this year when you moved to town. Who would have thought that the new pharmacist would have a son. My sister planned to capture you, seeing as how you were the richest boy in town, but you looked right past her and started talking to me. I thanked the lord that I never stopped going to church and I was there to meet you. You talked to me and told me how much you hated those stupid silly girls who only wanted to get married, like my sister. You told me how pretty I was and I believed you and I still do believe you. Only now that is the problem.

Radium Girls

Dolores Whiskeyman

Scene: Orange, New Jersey, 1928

Dramatic

Grace (twenty-six), soft-spoken, shy; once a top-notch dial painter at the
U.S. Radium Corporation.

*Grace has been fatally poisoned by working in the radium plant. As she waits
for her turn to testify against her employers, she laments the future she will
never have.*

GRACE: Can I tell you what I really want? Even more than the money?

[WILEY: Of course.]

GRACE: I want them to look at me. Mrs. Wiley I want them to see me — and
see what they did. So they can't hide any more.

[WILEY: Then don't you let them, Grace. Don't let them hide.]

(Grace opens a curtain.)

GRACE: All my life, Mrs. Wiley. I've tried so hard to be good. And do what I
was told. My father says. Go to work at the radium plant, it pays a good
wage. So I do. Mrs. MacNeil says put that brush in your mouth to get a
point. So I do. I never say, this paint tastes funny. Even though it does.
I never say, please can't I stay in school? But at night, I'd lie here and imagine what it would be like when Tommy and I got married and I could
have my own home and make my own decisions. And then I'd look over
at my dress hanging on the back of the door, all aglow — my shoes on
the floor, my hairbrush on the dresser. So much light. And I never ques-
tioned. So much light!

The Reindeer Biters

Jussi Wahlgren

Scene: Here and now
Serio-Comic
Eva (fifties), an embittered university professor.

> *Here, Eva leaves a rather pathetic message on a young friend's answering machine.*

EVA: *(Enters the front of the stage with a mobile.)* I was once accused of being too soft with a student when he had copied an assignment from somebody else. It happened in the early seventies. It was the Hippie time, flowers and peace and all that bull. He slept with me and I felt grateful. I never realized that men pay and pay and pay all their lives for having a penis . . . It's true. I am the fucking female with the treasure and that's what they are after. Like my late husband Markus. He cried when we did it for the first time. That's why I married him. He had feelings. He showed them. That's what I thought . . . What an asshole I was. When I'm gone, who cares who did what with whom and how many times. I'm just gone. It's a horrible thought. Nobody gives a shit . . . Do you know what I mean, Kris? I know it sounds pathetic but, by God, that's what it is! . . . I bet you're doing it right now. Is it Patrick or Phillip? Or the taxi driver. When I see you Kris I see myself thirty years ago. Shit *(Cries slowly.)* . . . Sorry, I dropped the joint. It's not what you do but what other people think you're doing. Do you understand what I'm saying. You have to be a super human being to listen to your heart. I don't think it's even possible . . . I'm not saying that it's all so bad either, but . . . What the fuck am I talking to a bloody machine . . . *(Exits.)*

Romeo & Juliet Part II
Sandra Hosking

Scene: The home of Romeo and Juliet
Serio-Comic
Juliet (twenty to thirty), a woman disillusioned with her marriage.

Here, disquiet Juliet wonders if she should have married her Romeo.

JULIET: Good, they are gone. I pray Friar Lawrence can draw my husband into this present time. Sometimes methinks his mind remains entombed. Aye me. My back bears the weight of a hundred horses galloping up and down upon it. *(Talking to her stomach.)* I am ready for you. Your bed is made with wool blankets. A dozen sisters await you. How nice a present it would be to have you to wake up to. If you do not. I shall have to cut you out. *(Contraction.)* Oh! *(Relaxes.)*

(She takes a shiny urn off of a shelf.) Oh, Nurse, how I wish you were here in person. *(Looks at her reflection.)* Oh. I am aged. How tired I look. Where is that maiden of yesteryear? She is in the faces of my little ones.

Kind, sweet, Nurse. My problem now is not my physical state. It is a matter of the heart. It is my Romeo. I fear he no longer loves me. He thinks me fat and old and a crank. Now I know why Mama and Papa maintain separate quarters.

And this, dear Nurse, I cannot bear. He speaks in his sleep. I have not told him thus, for things said in sleep are not meant for the light of day, though they eventually have a way of finding illumination. The other night he called out a name . . . Rosaline. I cannot discount this utterance. She was his unrequited love. What or why he thinks of her I know not, but my mind is wrought with torturous wondering. I'm afraid my obsession has turned me into a shrew.

If you were here, you could tell me not to worry. That I am his only true love. That I am the one he comes home to each day after his meanderings.

Here is the rub. I, too, dream of another time. 'Tis hard to remember our humble beginnings. When to be apart was like moving the tide back with a spoon. I cannot help but wonder what life would have been like had I married Paris. Mother reminds me of it each time I see her. Perhaps if I would not have chosen Romeo, I would not have fallen out of my father's favor. And perhaps I would have a big house overlooking Verona such as the thin, fair Rosaline.

'Tis no good to think of these things. Thank you, Nurse. Even in death, you comfort me.

Sisters
Gabriel Lanci

Scene: Here and now
Dramatic
Jeanine (forty to fifty), a disillusioned parent.

Here, Jeanine offers insight into the bittersweet nature of being a mom.

JEANINE: I've learned that there are some moments in a mother's life that can't be measured in terms of happiness. A child grows away from you and you're sent to the sidelines. He doesn't want you in the game anymore; you just have to watch from a distance. But there are times when that distance is reduced and he calls you in for a quick consultation: perhaps on his marriage day or when his first child is born. Children want to be assured that they've done the right thing. So of course they go to you for approval. And if you don't approve *(Beat.)* they know something must be wrong *(Beat.)* with you, that you're getting older, or senile, or just ornery. *(Beat.)* Kids do things when they become adults, things you've already done for them. They want to be "reborn" and prove that they can do it better than their mothers can. And of course it's not as good, and they call you to come and fix it for them. And you go, like the mother you are, to make it better, or go away, or *(2 Beats.)*. There is no reward *(Beat.)* being a mother all your life. You've got to look for happiness *(Beat.)* someplace else. When you leave their lives go, and never look back. And when they want you back they should be charged a fee for your readmission. And what would that be? Well, think of this. All his life, as he grew up, you were there, planning, building, making smooth the rough places for him to move forward into the world he wanted to be in. You made sacrifices that he will never know about, and it would be useless to tell him because he would say it was totally unnecessary, he could have done it himself. And that is the point of pain, after you struggled and scraped together the little you have for him, he says, "Why did you do that? I could have done it myself." *(Beat.)* Well you didn't Buster! Your mother did it for you, and she deserves some recognition for it! *(2 beats.)* So give it to her, while she's here to enjoy it *(Beat.)* and everything will be — fine.

Sisters

Gabriel Lanci

Scene: Here and now
Dramatic
Jesse (forty to fifty), a woman facing death.

Here, dying Jesse laments the fact that she never had children of her own.

JESSE: This must be the end of my life. It's funny, you don't realize it after it happens to you. I have to keep reminding myself that I have no place to go, no business, no activity, no thoughts, no feelings. Is this the way it should be? *(Beat.)* I'm not worried, I'm not sad in fact I feel very, very happy. Why am I so happy? I don't know where I'm going and my life was such a loss. *(Beat.)* One regret I have now is that I never gave life to anyone. There is no one there with my genes in them, no one with my identity, no child of mine. *(Beat.)* I wanted children, I don't know why I never got them. There was nothing wrong with Joe or me, we should have had children and we tried to. I envied my sister. Can we talk about sin here? I don't understand my life. I wanted so much to be a mother, to have children and watch them grow up and have their own children. Joe and I sincerely wanted that. But we never got it. Jeanie on the other hand, was given children, and she let them go, gave them away, abandoned them, I don't know what to call it. And after that, she got more children. What was that? Talk about unfairness! Do we ever get to ask God why these things were done? *(Beat.)* Now should be the time. *(Beat.)* Before I go any further, I want to know. What did I do wrong? What great sin kept me from becoming a parent? With all the injustices of the world, all the inflicted pain and desolation why does God do it? If there was something else He wanted me to do with my life, He should have told me. No messages, no visions, no voices, nothing. I bet Jeanine wherever she is thinks this is funny. *(Beat.)* What are you telling me? *(Beat.)* I remind you of your son Tony? Is that what you're saying? God knows I taught him how to think. The poor kid would have been totally lost without anyone who knew what he was going through. All that despair he carried around inside could have destroyed him. He could have bombed out on drugs and alcohol or something else, but he didn't. I taught him how to be angry, and get that anger out there where everybody could see it! That's what he needed — to show his feelings, not keep them bottled up and obedient. It got him through *(Beat.)* you. *(Beat.)* We tried to give each other so much, but we didn't need that. We should have reached inside of ourselves and pulled out the longing and the fear and the despair and looked at them for what they really are *(Beat.)* hope gone astray, dreams we've awakened in the middle of and don't know how they end. Now he'll always wonder, and he'll always fear knowing *(Beat.)* why. *(Jesse turns to go. Upstage has become a large black space as she moves slowly upstage into the darkness.)* But, in the end it hasn't been too bad, Jeanie, has it?

Teotwaki

Jo J. Adamson

Scene: A casino
Serio-Comic
Bertha (fifties), a woman just beginning to live life.

Here, Bertha shares the sad story of her marriage to Oscar, an insensitive boor, with her sister slot-machine players.

BERTHA: I started collecting stuffed bears the year I married. My husband was a supervisor at the sawmill and I was alone a lot of the time. Come to think of it, he wasn't much company when he was there. He just watched TV, ate and slept.

You always remember the first in a collection.
Of bears, that is. Not husbands.

(Bertha giggles a little.)

My first was a brown bear stuffed with excelsior. He had a embroidered nose. I called him "Wooly." I paid twenty dollars for him and that was a lot of the money in the 1960's.

Wooly sat on my bed, until Oscar, my husband, took him off. Every time he saw it he thought that the neighbor's longhaired cat had sneaked in and was sleeping on the bed.

He hated anything that was fluffy and moved. After Wooly, I bought "Divinity." He was twelve inches long and had pure white fur with pellets and poly stuffing. I didn't think anything could be as soft as Divinity.

Every six months, I added another bear to my collection. I bought angel bears, mafia bears, pirate bears, frog bears, baseball bears, football bears, panda bears, chef bears, Santa Claus bears, and even a Hell's Angel bear.

By the time I was fifty I had 100 bears on the big shelf in the hall.

Oscar told me that the weight of the bears on the shelf would break it. The shelf was strong enough for his handgun collection, I pointed out. "Say, Bertie, you've given me an idea," he said. "I could convert that shelf into a gun display case. Get rid of the bears."

I thought he'd just forget about building the display case — most nights he wasn't home. He'd developed quite an appetite for Porterhouse steaks. It was Easter Sunday. I had just returned after visiting my mother in Wenatchee and went upstairs to unpack my clothes.
It was then I saw it. The display rack. My bears were nowhere to be seen. I didn't want to interrupt the 6 o'clock news, it makes him mad when I do that. I waited until supper to ask him about the bears.

"Oscar," I said, " What did you do with my bear collection?" He reached for the roast beef. "What are you talking about, Woman?"
"The bears that I've been collecting since we married. Where are they?"

"Bears? — Oh them. Don't you think you're a little old to play with teddy bears?" He jabbed at the roast with his fork and put it to his mouth. "I don't play with them," I said trying to keep my voice steady. "I collect them."

(As Bertha talks she "plays" with the little bear. Bouncing him up and down, stroking his fur, etc.)

"Bertie," he says, as he scooped up some mashed potatoes on his spoon. "I gave them to the little girl down the street. You know, the one with MS."

Now, I know Oscar. He hasn't given anything away since our daughter got married. "Seriously, Oscar. What did you do with my bears?"

"Don't worry, your little bears have gone to a happier place." He poured some ketchup on the beef, picked up a parker house roll, and just as he was about to butter his roll, I lost it.

"What did you do with my friggin' bears, you sonofabitch!"

(Emma and Hannah can only stare at Bertha. They were not expecting such language.)

(Beat.)

[HANNAH: What did the sonofabitch do with the friggin' bears?]

(Bertha puts the bear back on the slot machine. She sighs.)

BERTHA: He donated them to the Marine Corps' "Toys for Tots" program.

Anyway, after he left me for "Medium Rare" I stopped collecting things. I figured I didn't need all that stuff collecting dust. Besides, I learned that there was a whole world outside of my door. I joined the YWCA, took pottery and watercolor classes — even joined a poetry group. I met other women like myself who were divorced, and I even started to travel on tour buses. Like the one that took me here, to the "Win-A-Lot" casino.

Oscar never let me wear pants. He said no woman of his was going to be seen in trousers. Even when all the women started to wear them, he wouldn't let me buy a pair.

A few months after he left, I went out and bought myself a bright red pantsuit with a matching scarf.

Teotwaki

Jo J. Adamson

Scene: A casino
Serio-Comic
Hannah (fifties), a woman who finds happiness where she can.

> *Hannah here explains why she chose to remain in a loveless marriage with a man with whom she has nothing in common.*

HANNAH: I never tried to torch my bra, but I once joined
a feminist group. The book discussion group was full and
I was feeling a little uneasy with my life and so I
thought I'd give it a go.

My husband asked what I wanted to
join a group of hysterical females.

Well, there wasn't a 'hysterical' female in the lot. But there were plenty of angry females, and frustrated females, and females who wore no makeup or bras. These women wanted something more than marriage, kids, and a mortgage. They wanted to 'find themselves!'

I made fun of them. "Find yourselves? Why, are you lost?" I become sarcastic when I'm uneasy. And these women made me very uneasy.

One woman suggested that they might threaten me.

"Threaten me? Don't be absurd," I said. "I'm a happily married woman with a full life."

"If that's true, why are you here?"

I like to read, I said lamely. The truth of the matter was I didn't know why I was there. There was a big empty hole around my heart, and I wanted to fill it up. I was becoming invisible, and I wanted people to see me.

When I tried to tell Henry what transpired in the sessions, it sounded so silly. Phrases like "my own space" "my own body" tripped off my tongue until I felt like the walking feminist bible, "Our Body Ourselves."

I misquoted Gloria Steinem and Germaine Greer. I told Henry he was as worthless as a fish on a bicycle. That I'd dwindled into a wife, and if men had to have abortions, it would become a sacrament.

I spewed out all the rhetoric of the women's movement as if it were divine law and before long I had stopped wearing a bra and I'd let my hair go back to its natural color. Gray.

Henry was beside himself. What did I want? A divorce? A Hawaiian vacation? A trip to Las Vegas, what?

I wasn't 'fulfilled,' I said. That was the other 'F' word in the 80's.

Henry finally gave me an ultimatum — choose that militant women's group or him. I couldn't have both.

My last meeting was on a Halloween night. We were having a little party and I came as a Humpty Dumpty. It somehow fit.

"Trick or Treat," I said after we downed a bottle of Merlot. "I'm outa here."

What have we done? Are we too extreme? Many of them were divorced or had alternative life styles . . .

(Hannah looks at Bertha.)

. . . that means they have sleepovers with their girlfriends, Bertha.

[BERTHA: I know what a lesbian is. I watched "Ellen" come out on national TV!]

HANNAH: Why was I leaving the group, they demanded. I had learned a lot and had opened myself up to them.

I thought long and hard about it, and then it hit me.

I was leaving because if I stayed I would have to admit that my entire life — my marriage, my children, and my friendships was one big lie. If those women knew what they were talking about, my life would be invalid. Unjustifiable, and irrelevant: it would have no more meaning than an expired driver's license.

"I am forty-five years old. Too old to want my own space." Shoot, I didn't even know we *had* our own space. Mine was always full of *people.*

I left the group and like Humpty Dumpty remained sitting on the wall. I wasn't happy and I wasn't unhappy. I was just . . . present and accounted for.

When Henry retired, we found out that we didn't have much in common. We didn't have much to say to one another. Hell, I'm not even sure we even like one another.

He does his thing, golf, and I do mine, play games, and never the twain should meet. I hate golf and he wouldn't be caught dead inside of a casino.

Tony Nutcracker

Jocelyn Beard

Scene: Here and now
Serio-Comic
Woman (any age).

A woman who's bored with Ballanchine.

WOMAN: There comes a time in every woman's life when she really has to ask herself: "Is it possible that I've seen 'The Nutcracker' one too many times?" I mean, I was fast asleep by the time they got to the Land of the Sweets last time. Sitting right there in the New York State Theatre in Lincoln Center. Snoring. Not caring that I was snoring. Really kind of proud. I used to resent the hell out of those businessmen who get dragged to Lincoln Center year after year by their wives slash girlfriends who just settle into their seats and start sawing wood. But now I sympathize. Who can blame them, or me for that matter? The Nutcracker is tired. Watching it makes you tired. By the time the mice attack, my mind's on last Sunday's episode of *The Sopranos*. Tchaikovsky should have taken a page out of David Chase's book. The Silberhauses could be like the Sopranos, Frau Silberhaus and Herr Silberhaus are Carmella and Tony. Clara and Fritz are Meadow and AJ. That freak Dr. Drosselmeyer is Paulie Walnuts and the Sugar Plum Fairy is the shrink with the legs. The Nutcracker is some hot young wise guy that Meadow's in love with. When the wiseguy Nutcracker sneaks into the Silberhaus house on Christmas Eve, Fritz — slash — AJ pops him with his brand new .9 mm that his dad just gave him, but he's a lousy shot. Paulie Drosselmeyer pulls the bullet out the kid's ass and Clara aka Meadow grabs the gun and shoots Fritz — bam — dead. Then, the mice — who are like the Feds — break into the house to try and wire the whole place for sound. Clara and the Nutcracker blast the Feds to kingdom come. This wakes up her mom, who gets really pissed about blood all over the new wallpaper. When her dad, Tony Silberhaus, gets home from his job at the Bada-Bing Cherry, he slaps the shit out of Fritz, who isn't really dead, just stunned. Then, Silberhaus and Drosselmeyer decide to get Clara and the Nutcracker out of New Jersey fast, so they send them to upstate New York in a snowstorm, where members of an Asian gang try to kill them. Silberhaus shows up and caps all the Asians, then the Sugar Plum Fairy shows up with her son — who's a senior at Bard College — and gives them all huge quantities of Prozac and Zoloft, which makes them all feel better about everything they've done. After he feels better, Tony Silberhaus fucks a Snowflake, which pisses off the Sugar Plum Fairy. Clara Meadow decides that the Nutcracker isn't as hot as the Sugar Plum Fairy's son — who is much more sensitive than the Nutcracker and is, of course, a Bard student. This pisses off the Nutcracker, who makes a pass at the Sugar Plum Fairy who finally gives in to her animal lust and bangs the Nutcracker in an effort to make Herr Silberhaus jealous. Silberhaus finds out and wacks the Nutcracker. Drosselmeyer calls to say that The Nutcracker and Clara have been cleared of all charges concerning the death of the mice, so they all go home to New Jersey, except for the Sugar Plum Fairy's kid, who goes back to Bard. Silberhaus lies to Drosselmeyer about the Nutcracker and says that he got jacked by one of the Asians. Frau Carmella Silberhaus is pissed because she's found out about the Snowflake, who was from Russia. Silberhaus tries to make it up to her by scoring her a huge diamond from the Land of Sweets, and that seems to do the trick — but with Frau Silberhaus, you never really know. *(Pause.)* It works for me.

Too Direct

Jeff Goode

Scene: A theater
Serio-Comic
Kris (twenties), an auditioning actress.

Here, an overeager actress overstates her case at an audition.

KRIS: Hi.

You probably don't remember me.

I mean, of course you don't, why would you?

But I was at a show you did, like, jeez, a year ago.

A friend of mine — Do you know Casey?

(Tiny pause, no response, move on.)

Right anyway. It was her idea.

I think she worked on it maybe, or she works here?

(Tiny pause.)

Never mind, doesn't matter. But so that's why I was here.

And they had that thing afterwards where everybody was just hanging out, and so that's where it was.

(Looks uncomfortable.)

Can I just — ?

(Climbs down off the stage.)

I hate being onstage.

But I heard you were having auditions and my friends were like "Go, go, you have to do this."

And so I don't know if this is weird or . . .
No, it is. It's weird, I know. It is, it's weird.
But the thing is — Can I just say one thing?

(Moving a little closer to the director.)

I don't know if you remember this, but there was this guy, the lead guy,
you were talking to, big guy, I don't know his name.
And I don't know what he said or what you guys were talking about . . .
But you just went off on him.
You were just "And this, and this, and this, and this!"
And he was like, completely, had no idea.
And everyone was like . . . wow.
You were just so . . . Confident.
You were like . . . on fire with it. It was amazing.
And I was just "Who IS that??"
And I know this is stupid, and I know this isn't what you want to hear
right now while you're doing all this,
I know you're busy. But I'm not an actor, so I don't know how I'm ever
going to even get a chance to even
BE here just to say . . .

(Looking the director in the eye.)

I would give anything. To be here.
Right now.
Like this.
With you.

The Trestle At Pope Lick Creek

Naomi Wallace

Scene: A town outside an American city, 1936

Dramatic

Gin (forty-one), a woman whose world is irrevocably changed when her
   son, Dalton, is arrested for the murder of Pace, a young woman who
   had recently been obsessed with Dalton's struggle to find identity.

*After returning home from another exhausting day from the factory, Gin here
shares the following anecdote with Pace's ghost.*

GIN: Oh. Pace.

(Pace is still. She just watches Gin.)

GIN: I didn't see you. I was just. Trying to get used to this. It won't come off.
   They're lights, almost. It doesn't hurt. Well, it hurts cause I scrub them
   but it does no good. This color's here to stay. One morning I go to work
   and I come home with blue hands. They changed chemicals again at the
   plant. All sixteen of us in my section got blue hands. Some of the women,
   they were upset when it wouldn't wash off. But we had to see it as a wonder, too. During break, we turned off the lights and standing all together,
   some with our arms raised, others at our side, we looked like a Christmas tree in the dark, with blue lights. Then we all put our arms over our
   heads like this *(Demonstrates.)* and waved our fingers and we were a flock
   of crazy blue birds taking off. We started laughing then, and piling on
   top of each other, imagine it, and most of us women my age, and our
   hands were like blue snowballs flying this way and that. One of the girls,
   Victoria, she laughed so hard she peed right where she stood. Another
   one, Willa, she slipped in it and that had all of us roaring. *(Beat.)* Then
   Laura Townsend said we all had better think again cause we had the hands
   of dead women. Well, that put an end to the fun and we went back to
   work. The manager said it would wear off but it won't. We even used
   bleach. We'll have to get used to it. Kind of ugly and kind of pretty both,
   isn't it? But hands aren't meant to be blue.

The Victorian Traveler

Linda Stockham

Scene: The late nineteenth century

Dramatic

Malta "Molly" Blackburn (forty to sixty), a Victorian woman fortunate
  enough to have traveled the world.

*Here, Molly recalls the solitude that sustained her during her years of travel-
ing the globe and the revelations enjoyed in the process.*

MALTA "MOLLY" BLACKBURN: Father died in 1868 on our second trip to New
  Zealand. I didn't know how ill he was. He died in Auckland of a liver
  ailment. It happened quickly; it happened too quickly. I was not prepared.
  (Crying.)
  After my father's death I discovered that I traveled best to the tune
  of the solitary pilgrim. I found that it was in my nature to live and work
  detached from others, particularly any British residents in the countries
  I visited. I discovered this the first time I traveled after my father's death.
  I felt more at home in a shanty for £4 per month than any convenient
  fellow-countryman's home away from home. I wanted my physical and
  emotional distance from England. I wanted my solitude. I wanted and
  did set my world upon many verandas, my evenings there after being in
  the field sketching and painting, enjoying the night noises while drinking the local beverage. In South America it was *mate* and in Tibet it was
  salted and buttered tea. Sometimes the beverage was bitter, sometimes
  sweet, but almost always it was strong and invigorating. Some drinks
  would take a lifetime to acquire a taste for, others instantly delightful to
  the tongue. But I always was willing to try them. Mostly I lived upon
  bread and butter and whatever local fruits and vegetables were available.
  I never ate meat. Fish, on occasion, but never meat. Never mammal. I
  stepped into jungles, climbed great mountains, walked across high plains
  and sensed the sacred places where time was asleep. It was all-primal where
  I stepped away from my presence and touched my second soul. For fleet-
  ing moments I saw all there had been and was enraptured in being part
  of the past. It had nothing to do with creation, the gods, or distance. It

had to do with the moment and me; that is, before human life encroached upon and eroded away the beauty of paradise like an all-consuming flood. This I found in my travels but lost in England, that place where I was an empty woman.

When They Speak of Rita
Daisy Foote

Scene: Here and now
Dramatic
Rita (forty to fifty), a woman in the midst of a mid-life crisis.

> *Following a disastrous affair with a younger man, Rita finds herself back in the thick of her unfulfilling life. Here she laments the fact that she has never been good at anything.*

RITA: I was reading this article on Frisbee throwers.
   (Jeannie moves over to the table.)
[JEANNIE: Frisbee throwers?]
RITA: Did you know that there are actual competitions for this sort of thing?
[JEANNIE: No.]
RITA: These people in the tournaments are really good. They can perform hundreds of tricks with the Frisbee. And there's a lot of prize money to win, they're even trying to get it in the Olympics. There are so many things in this world a person can be good at. It's just a matter of finding something and really working at it.
[JEANNIE: Like you and cooking.]
RITA: That's not the same thing. I just do a few simple things well. But as far as anything fancy, anything requiring real skill, I have no ability.
   (A beat.)
   When I was with Jimmy, I went to apply for a job at this catering operation. They practically laughed at me when I told them about my experience, they were looking for a professional, someone who can carve swans out of cheese dip. Cooking meals for my family didn't count. The only job available for me was bussing tables —
RITA: What would you say you were good at?

When They Speak of Rita

Daisy Foote

Scene: Here and now

Dramatic

Rita (forty to fifty), a woman in the midst of a mid-life crisis.

Here, Rita confronts her husband, Asa, with the full depth of her emptiness and despair.

RITA: Right before I graduated from high school I was having supper with my mother and father, my father asks me about my plans for the future.
(*A beat.*)
And then my mother says, "Maybe you'll marry Asa." So I nodded, and that was that.
(*A beat.*)
We got married. Then I got pregnant with Warren and every day this restless feeling in me would grow. I would sit in this kitchen and wait for something to happen. I would wait for an idea to come to me about what to do, but it never came.
(*A beat.*)
I was so sure when Jeannie said she was pregnant and giving up college to marry Warren — I was so sure she'd end up feeling the way that I do. But she doesn't. She seems content. And I think she'll always be content. I don't understand that, why is she so content and I'm not? Why do you think that is, Asa?

[ASA: I don't know.]

RITA: When people see me now, when they speak of me, I know most of them talk about what a sad, foolish woman I am. And while that makes me want to hide in the house and avoid people, avoid their eyes, I don't know how I'll feel if they stop talking to me, if everything goes back to the way it was before.
(*A beat.*)
Some day, years from now, when I'm in the graveyard and someone happens to see my name on a gravestone they'll ask, "Rita Potter, who was

Rita Potter?" Then they'll move on and my name will slip from their minds. And really it will be like I was never here at all.

(A beat.)

I suppose most people don't worry about that. Do you ever worry about it?

ALASKA Copyright 1999 by Le Wilhelm
Reprinted by Permission of the Author
Contact Cynthia Granville, 162 Nesbit, Weehawken, NJ 0705, 201-601-2431

AND THE WINNER IS . . .Copyright 2000 by David-Matthew Barnes
Reprinted by Permission of the Author
Contact The Dorothy Nickle Performing Arts Company, 2221 West Giddings Street,
    Chicago, IL 60625, Attention: Harriet Russell, Literary Department

ANTON IN SHOW BUSINESS by Jane Martin, Copyright 2000 by Alexander Speer,
    Trustee
Reprinted by Permission of Alexander Speer, Trustee,
Contact Samuel French

APARTMENT 3A Copyright 2000 by Jeff Daniels
Reprinted by Permission of International Creative Management
CAUTION: APARTMENT 3A, being duly copyrighted is subject to a royalty. The
Dramatists Play Service, Inc., 440 Park Avenue South, New York, NY 10016. No professional or non-professional performance of the play (excluding first-class professional
performance) may be given without obtaining in advance the written permission of
the Dramatists Play Service, Inc. and paying the requisite fee. Inquiries concerning all
other rights should be addressed to Sarah Jane Leigh, ICM, 40 West 57th Street, New
York, NY 10019.

ASYLUM Copyright 2000 by Kara Hartzler
Reprinted by Permission of the Author
Contact Kara Hartzler, 1951 Delta Avenue, West Branch, IA 52358, *KaraHartz@aol.com*

BACK STORY "Maid of Athens" by David Rambo, based on characters created by
Joan Ackermann, Copyright 2001 by the Actors Theatre of Louisville
Reprinted by Permission of The Actors Theatre of Louisville
For Information Contact Dramatic Publishing

BAD PARTY Copyright 2000 by Alison Diana Meehan
Reprinted by Permission of the Author
Contact: Beast Mountain, (845) 878-9898

BE MY BABY! by Michele Forsten Copyright 2000 by Michele Forsten
Reprinted by Permission of the Author
Contact: Michele Forsten, 59 West 88th Street #1R, New York, NY 10024-2545, *mich@bway.net*

BETTY'S SUMMER VACATION Copyright 1999 by Christopher Durang
Reprinted by Permission of Grove Press
For Performance Rights: Helen Merrill, Ltd., 295 Lafayette Street, New York, NY 10012

BIG LOVE Copyright 2000 by Charles L. Mee
Reprinted by Permission of International Creative Management
For Information: Libby Edwards, ICM, 40 West 57th Street, New York, NY 10019

BIG POTATO Copyright by Arthur Laurents
Reprinted by Permission of William Morris Agency, Inc. on behalf of the Author. CAU-TION: Professionals and amateurs are hereby warned that BIG POTATO by Arthur Laurents is subject to a royalty. It is fully protected under the copyright laws of the United States of America, and of all countries covered by the International Copyright Union (including the Dominion of Canada and the rest of the British Commonwealth), and of all countries covered by the Pan-American Copyright Convention and the Universal Copyright Convention, the Berne Convention and of all countries with which the United States has reciprocal copyright relations. All rights, including professional, amateur/motion picture stage rights, recitation, lecturing, public reading, radio broadcasting, television, video or sound recording, all other forms of mechanical or electronic reproduction, such as CD-ROM, CD-1, information storage and retrieval systems and photocopying, and the rights of translation into foreign languages, are strictly reserved. Particular emphasis is laid on the question of readings, permission for which must be secured from the author's agent in writing. Inquiries concerning rights should be addressed to: William Morris Agency, Inc., 1325 Avenue of the Americas, New York, NY 10019, Attn: Peter Franklin

BLUE MOVIE Copyright 2000 by Jay Boyer
Reprinted by Permission of the Author
For Information: Jay Boyer, Creative Writing Program, Department of English, Arizona State University, Tempe, AZ 85287-0302

CLAUDIA LAZLO Copyright by Arthur Laurents
Reprinted by Permission of William Morris Agency, Inc. on behalf of the Author. CAU-TION: Professionals and amateurs are hereby warned that CLAUDIA LAZLO by Arthur Laurents is subject to a royalty. It is fully protected under the copyright laws

THE MEMORY OF WATER Copyright 1997 by Shelag Stephenson
Reprinted by Permission of The Gersh Agency
Contact Peter Hagan, The Gersh Agency, 130 West 42nd Street, New York, NY 10036,
212-634-8115

MRS. MYGOODNESS Copyright 2000 by David Fleisher
Reprinted by Permission of the Author
For Information contact David Fleisher, 4130 Tivoli Court #302, Lake Worth, FL
33467, 561-965-9723, *dfleis1662@aol.com*

NUDE MONOLOGUE Copyright 2000 by Jeff Goode
Reprinted by Permission of the Author
Contact Jeff Goode, 1501 Brentwood Lane, Wheaton, IL 60187, *JeffGoode@aol.com,
www.jeffgoode.com*

THE ONE Copyright 2000 by Jolene Goldenthal
Reprinted by Permission of the Author
Contact Jolene Goldenthal, 17 Wright Drive, Avon, CT 06001 or Susan Schulman,
434 West 44th Street, New York, NY 10036

PAST TENSE FEMININE GENDER Copyright 2000 by Le Wilhelm
Reprinted by Permission of the Author
Contact Cynthia Granville, 162 Nesbit, Weehawken, NJ 07057, 201-601-2431

POMPEI Copyright 2000 by Bob Jude Ferrante
Reprinted by Permission of the Author
Contact Bob Jude Ferrante, 616 East 19th Street, Brooklyn, NY 11230, (718) 421-
6977

PRETTY Copyright 2000 by Alison Diana Meehan
Reprinted by Permission of the Author
Contact Beast Mountain, 845-878-9898

RADIUM GIRLS Copyright 2000 by Dolores Whiskeyman
Reprinted by Permission of the Author
Contact Dolores Whiskeyman, P.O. Box 10643, Arlington, VA 22201

THE REINDEER BITERS Copyright 1999 by Jussi Wahlgren
Reprinted by Permission of the Author
For International Performing Rights contact: Charles Aerts, Theatre Productions,